Peking 1900

The Boxer Rebellion

Campaign • 85

Peking 1900

The Boxer Rebellion

Peter Harrington • Illustrated by Alan & Michael Perry

Series editor Lee Johnson • *Consultant editor* David G Chandler

First published in Great Britain in 2001 by Osprey Publishing, Midland
House, West Way, Botley, Oxford OX2 0PH, UK
443 Park Avenue South, New York, NY 10016, USA
Email: info@ospreypublishing.com

CIP Data for this publication is available from the British Library

ISBN-13: 978-1-84176-181-7

Editor: Lee Johnson
Design: The Black Spot
Indexer: Alan Rutter
Maps by The Map Studio
3D bird's eye views by The Black Spot
Battlescene artwork by Alan & Michael Perry
Origination by PPS Grasmere Ltd., Leeds, UK
Printed in China through World Print Ltd.
Typeset in Helvetica Neue and ITC New Baskerville

08 09 10 11 12   16 15 14 13 12 11 10 9 8 7

FOR A CATALOGUE OF ALL BOOKS PUBLISHED BY
OSPREY MILITARY AND AVIATION PLEASE CONTACT:

NORTH AMERICA
Osprey Direct, C/o Random House Distribution Center,
400 Hahn Road, Westminster, MD 21157, USA
E-mail: info@ospreydirect.com

ALL OTHER REGIONS
Osprey Direct UK, P.O. Box 140, Wellingborough,
Northants, NN8 2FA, UK
E-mail: info@ospreydirect.co.uk

www.ospreypublishing.com

Dedication

I would like to dedicate this book to Frederic A. Sharf
who has been a constant source of inspiration and
encouragement to me.

Acknowledgments

I would like to acknowledge the Jean S. and Frederic A.
Sharf Collection for supplying many of the original
photographs used in this publication. Information on the
battlefield today was supplied by Mr. James Hoare of the
British Foreign and Commonwealth Office, London, to
whom I am most grateful.

Artist's note

Readers may care to note that the original paintings from
which the colour plates in this book were prepared are
available for private sale. All reproduction copyright
whatsoever is retained by the Publishers. All enquiries
should be addressed to:

Michael Perry
26 Fishpond Drive
The Park
Nottingham
NG7 1DG

The Publishers regret that they can enter into no
correspondence upon this matter.

KEY TO MILITARY SYMBOLS

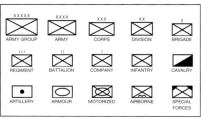

CONTENTS

BACKGROUND TO THE SIEGE OF PEKING

LEFT **The last stand of the Chinese at Langfang drawn by Frank Craig from a sketch by a British naval officer, and published in the *Graphic* on 25 August 1900. According to the officer who made the sketch, the train carrying around 900 British and Germans was attacked as it was going down to Yangtsun. The fighting lasted two hours and the scene shows Chinese troops trying unsuccessfully to save their banner. (Anne S.K. Brown Military Collection, Brown University Library)**

BELOW **The Chinese encampment in the North Fort at Taku on the Peiho River photographed in 1860. On 25 June 1860, the British bombarded the forts at Taku but landing parties were beaten back with heavy casualties. Two months later following a short bombardment, the North Fort was stormed by British and French troops, and the other forts quickly surrendered. Peking was entered on 12 October 1860. (Anne S.K. Brown Military Collection, Brown University Library)**

Simply put, the Boxer outbreak in North China in the summer of 1900 can be attributed directly to Chinese hatred of foreigners and foreign interference in their country. While there were other reasons for the revolt such as economic hardships brought on by poor harvests, floods and drought, they were all blamed on the 'foreign devils' who were encroaching on China in increasing numbers. In short, the Boxer Rebellion was a last gasp attempt to throw off the foreign yoke and preserve the Chinese culture, religion and way of life once and for all.

While the immediate causes can be traced to various events in 1898 and 1899, these were merely a culmination of over 60 years of Chinese frustration of mounting foreign interference in their country. Following the Napoleonic Wars, the victorious nations were looking to expand their foreign markets through the acquisition of foreign lands, a phenomenon that would only end with the First World War. Britain in particular looked towards China as an untapped resource worth exploiting and fought two wars between 1839 and 1860 in order to secure a foothold in the vast country. The first conflict, known today as the Opium War, lasted from 1839 until 1842 and was the result of disagreements between Chinese officials and British merchants in the port of Canton particularly concerning the supply of opium from India. Success was achieved by British forces with the capture of Shanghai and Chinkiangfoo in the summer of 1842 resulting in the Treaty of Nanking, in which Hong Kong was ceded to Britain, a war indemnity of $20 million was levied on the defeated, and various Chinese ports were opened up to British trade. Seventeen years later, a combined Anglo-French force attacked the Taku (Dagu) Forts at the mouth of the Peiho (Baihe) River in order to force the Chinese emperor to grant further trade concessions. Peking (Beijing) was entered by allied forces on 12 October 1860.

In the wake of the European military victories and the economic opportunities which they brought, came merchants and businessmen, arms dealers and engineers, missionaries and concessionaires, advisers and an odd assortment of unsavoury characters eager to make money at the expence of the Chinese. Both sides viewed the other with contempt, the Chinese poking fun at the physical characteristics of the Europeans such as their red hair and large noses, the Europeans seeing the Chinese as backward, racially inferior, and proof of Darwinian theories regarding the supremacy of the white race. The two sides did not mix well and the Europeans who moved into China created little enclaves where they lived apart from the Chinese. A few scholars and intellectuals tried to understand the natives by adapting to their dress and customs but the Chinese held them in contempt. The Catholic and Protestant churches felt it was their duty to 'civilise' the Chinese by introducing them to the Bible and the words of Jesus; and while they had some success in converting the local populations, most Chinese were highly cynical towards the Christian religion and ridiculed it. Both sides displayed absolute ignorance towards the other. Chinese reaction towards the foreigners took various forms, from violence and terrorism to passive resistance and xenophobic literature such as a publication entitled *The Death Blow to Corrupt Doctrines* in which the author poked fun at the Europeans in a derogatory fashion.

ANTI-FOREIGN RIOTS

It was in the southern provinces that the first anti-foreign incidents occurred during the decade 1886 to 1896. Earlier in 1875 a westerner had been murdered in Yunnan but it was the foreign presence in the south after 1884 which brought about the first significant developments. France had extended its empire into Tonkin by military conquest and the British were on China's border in Burma, and through a series of treaties both were allowed to build railways in China, obtain mining concessions, open up routes and create trading stations. In the wake of the traders and businessmen were the missionaries. It was too much for the Chinese at

Chungkung in Szechuan Province who destroyed the British consulate and other foreign buildings in July 1886. Three years later the foreign concession and consulates at Chinkiang were plundered and ruined by a Chinese mob. Next it was the turn of Hankow, where a riot led by students was swiftly put down, but these were just the beginning of a rapidly spreading movement which now began to attack Christian sites. A French Catholic orphanage was assailed but saved by French officials, and in May and June 1891 there were uprisings along the Yangtse River resulting in the death of several British citizens. While some of these attacks may have been spontaneous outpourings of Chinese hatred towards foreigners, there is evidence that some secret societies such as the anti-government *Kao Lao Hui* carried out attacks on missionaries hoping to embarrass the Manchus in Peking and bring about their fall. To many Chinese the Manchus were viewed as foreign usurpers – non-Chinese people from beyond the Great Wall who had conquered China as far back as 1644; they were to rule the country until their overthrow in 1912.

The overall impact of these disturbances was slight but they brought about a marked shift in the policies of the western powers who built up significant naval forces to patrol the region in the early 1890s at the same time making it very clear that they would not tolerate any further outrages committed against their citizens. Nonetheless, serious anti-foreign outbreaks occurred especially in the north, which up till then had been relatively immune from foreign incursions. Furthermore, in 1895 the various western missionary organisations made a concerted effort to bring the message to every Chinese, an act viewed by many as a portent of worse things to come.

SINO-JAPANESE WAR

Further evidence of foreign interference in Chinese affairs was Japan's invasion of Korea. This was in direct response to China's landing of 2,000 troops near Asan, Korea, on 10 June 1894 to suppress the Tonghaks, a group of Korean nationalists opposed to the Korean government. China regarded Korea as a satellite; by contrast Japan wanted the country under her sphere of influence in order to westernise and modernise it. The showdown on the Korean peninsula led to a humiliating defeat for China as Japan's western-trained and modelled army, and her British- and French-built ships proved more than a match for the large but ill-trained Chinese forces. After major defeats in September 1894 at Pyongyang and the Yalu River and in 1895 at Weihaiwei, the Chinese were forced to sue for peace and a treaty was signed at Shimonoseki on 17 April 1895. The victorious Japanese were granted concessions in China many of which were subsequently claimed by the other world powers. Large areas of the country had been devastated and many parts of the north were now subjected to occupation troops, resulting in serious economic disruptions and poor harvests. Compounding this were the thousands of returning Chinese soldiers who had not been paid and had no money, many of them resorting to crime to survive. Outrages against foreigners were on the rise in the north and there was an increase in membership of secret societies which actively sought out disgruntled veterans of the war.

While there was considerable anti-Japanese feeling in the north, this began to include all foreigners, who were regarded as the advance guard of a foreign invasion. There were rumours that missionaries had been seen importing and hiding cannon and stockpiling forage for the use of cavalry, but the cannon turned out to be galvanised iron stove pipes and the straw was for thatching. Nonetheless, it demonstrated the paranoia of the Chinese which was to some extent justified by the actions of the foreign powers. With China defeated and vulnerable they began to make more demands for special privileges, trade routes and railways, more mining concessions and even changes in the Chinese government. China had some success in resisting these demands but tensions developed in 1897 following the murder of two Germans in Shantung (Shandong) Province, a region identified as the centre of anti-foreign and anti-Christian activity. Germany was outraged and demanded territory as compensation. This presented Germany with the opportunity and excuse to finally secure a port on the Chinese coast and, sanctioned by the Kaiser, a German naval squadron occupied Kiaochow (Jiaozhou) Bay in Shantung Province forcing the Chinese to evacuate. To the Chinese, this was an outrage for this province had always been viewed as sacrosanct being the birthplace of Confucius.

Other nations could not stand by and watch Germany gain a naval foothold in China, and moved quickly to seize ports of their own. The Chinese were helpless to respond having virtually no navy following its annihilation in the war with Japan. Port Arthur was taken over by the Russians, Weihaiwei, also in Shantung Province, was occupied by the British, and the French took Kwangchowan in the south. Understandably, there was an overwhelming rise in anti-foreign and anti-Christian feelings among the Chinese. Nonetheless, the government in Peking was strong enough to dictate terms to the nations, referring to the new acquisitions as treaty ports which remained under Chinese control. On paper this was true but it did not stop hundreds of foreign administrators, businessmen, civilians and troops pouring into these ports. Trade increased dramatically through the treaty ports and the influx of imports such as cotton began to destabilise the Chinese domestic industry in the fabric. To make matters worse the importing of opium, which was forbidden by the government, was increasing.

Railways began to be constructed, churches sprang up, telegraph lines strung and mines sunk as foreign concessionaires began to make deals with the Chinese. Peking in particular became a centre for foreign concessionaires. It was all becoming too much for the Chinese and in a Secret Edict of 21 November 1899, the Dowager Empress stated, 'Let each strive to preserve from destruction and spoliation at the ruthless hands of the invader his ancestral home and graves. Let these our words be made known to each and all within our domain.' In fairness, it was not always easy for the foreigners to do business with the Chinese, who took every opportunity to insult and humiliate the westerners.

Anti-foreign agitation was on the rise, and within the diplomatic confines of the Legation Quarter in Peking a feeling of fear and concern for safety arose in late 1898, leading the foreign ambassadors to request that troops be sent up from the treaty ports to protect the Legations, and in October, 66 Russians, 30 Germans and 25 British guards arrived in the capital, the first foreign military presence in peacetime. Unwelcome by the Chinese, their presence did temper anti-foreign feelings in the capital for the time being.

THE EMERGENCE OF THE BOXERS

This was not the case in sacred Shantung Province, where the Boxers emerged along with several secret sects in the period following the end of the war with Japan. Their roots were in earlier sects such as the Big Sword Society which were pro-Chinese and distinctly anti-Manchu and developed in the rural villages, appealing particularly to idle young males with free time on their hands who normally would have been employed as farm workers but whom the drought and poor harvests had put out of work. The appeal may have been the physical exercise and public displays of martial arts which all members were expected to participate in. Boxing grounds were established around the country where performances were held to impress the populace and increase recruitment. One of the groups which emerged at the end of the 1890s and which opposed Christians was called 'Boxers United in Righteousness' (*Yihequan*); their slogan ran 'Support the Qing, destroy the foreigner'. They were a coalition of other boxing groups such as the Plum Flower Boxers (*Meihuaquan*), the Red Boxers (*Hongquan*), the Spirit Boxers (*Shenquan*) and others. Superstition and magic played an important part in the rites and their induced trance-like states, spirit processions and the swallowing of charms caught the imagination of rural Chinese. The Boxers claimed that once initiated their bodies were invulnerable to bullets and shells and demonstrations using blank bullets fired from muskets provided the necessary proof of their powers to the citizenry.

Their mass appeal was their call to exterminate all foreigners in China, particularly the Manchus, who were despised more for their inability to keep the country intact and the foreign powers at bay. While the Manchus were initially hostile to the Boxers, they came to believe more and more that the secret sect might be useful in achieving their ends of destroying foreign influence. By 1899 the Boxers were venting their anger towards native converts to Christianity and began a campaign of posting bulletins, placards and handbills denouncing Christianity. Their case was made even stronger as the poor harvests and constant droughts were blamed directly on the 'foreign devils'. The government tried to suppress the rebels, even attempting to transform them into militia to subsidise their depleted forces following the Sino-Japanese War. Pressure on the government to take action also came from the foreign community, and imperial troops from Qing Province were sent to put the Boxers down. The two sides clashed at Senluo Temple in the summer of 1899 and at least 27 Boxers were killed. This was also the first time that the Boxers referred to themselves as 'Militia United in Righteousness' (*Yihetuan*).

To date no foreign lives had been lost but this all changed on the last day of 1899 when a British missionary was murdered. Beyond a few diplomatic protests, the British took no further action other than to demand that the perpetrators be brought to justice as indeed they were

A Chinese Boxer Chief and his braves from a photograph published in July 1900. According to the caption, 'these Boxers, armed with the horrible jagged knife and the three-pronged fork, are typical of one class of our adversaries, those who yet have the primitive armament of barbaric times – evidently not passed away'. (Anne S.K. Brown Military Collection, Brown University Library)

in March 1900. At the same time, the openly anti-foreign governor of Shantung Province was replaced with an anti-Boxer strongman who brought things under control by early 1900. Unfortunately, his actions were only superficial and did not go to the root of the problem – the continuing anti-foreign feeling that was growing in the country. All the Boxers did was to move out of the province and by April 1900 had begun to establish themselves in the neighbouring province of Chihli (Zhili), one group heading towards Tientsin (Tianjin), the only treaty port which had a substantial foreign population, while another headed in the direction of the capital, Peking, where the Manchu government was exhibiting increasing pro-Boxer tendencies. Indeed on 11 January 1900, the Empress Dowager issued a proclamation stating that secret societies were woven into the very fabric of Chinese culture and should not be mistaken for criminal elements. Had the Boxers not been forced to quit Shantung, the rebellion might never have flared up.

As the Boxers moved into Chihli, all the while increasing in numbers, Christian communities were attacked in their wake. Recruitment grew as famine and drought began to grip Chihli Province, more foreign missionaries appeared in the countryside, and opposition grew to the new railway which had been built from Tientsin to the capital. The destruction of the latter offered a means to strike back at the foreigners. The proclamation of 11 January provided further impetus, for it claimed that Christians should be treated like any other troublesome group and dealt with as the law required. The Boxers took the apparent support of the Empress as carte blanche to undertake their murderous deeds.

In the government, it was also becoming apparent that the moderates such as Prince Ch'ing (Qing), who controlled the Tsungli (Zongli) Yamen or the Chinese Foreign Office, were gradually being replaced by the anti-foreign lobby composed of conservative Manchus, namely Prince Tuan and Jung-Lu, the former a close confidant of the Empress. Prince Tuan's son, P'u Chun, was named as her Heir Apparent, thereby usurping the power of the Emperor Kuang Hsü. It was an ill omen for the foreign community and the stage was set for a showdown as Prince Tuan began to openly encourage the Boxers despite numerous protests from the foreign ministers which fell on deaf ears.

More and more outrages were committed against foreigners in the spring of 1900. In the village of Chiang Chia Chuang near Paotingfu, a city 60 miles south-west of the capital, a force of poorly equipped Boxers estimated to be in the region of 2,000, attacked the mainly Roman Catholic community who had prepared for such an event by building defences, and were beaten off. But in mid-May, they got their revenge by attacking missions and Chinese Christians in the same area, killing 70 converts. As disturbances in Chihli Province spread, it was natural that the Boxers would come into contact with government troops and a series of engagements took place. Imperial troops under Colonel Yang Futong closed a boxing ground at Gaoluo on 15 May; on the following day he was ambushed but his force killed 60 Boxers. Some days later, the Boxers took the government forces by surprise and killed Yang. Shortly after a force of over 10,000 Boxers captured Zhouzhou on the railway line to the capital and on the 27th began to attack the railway, ripping up lines, destroying bridges and stations and cutting telegraph lines. On the 29th, the court issued instructions to 'annihilate Boxers who refused to disperse', but this

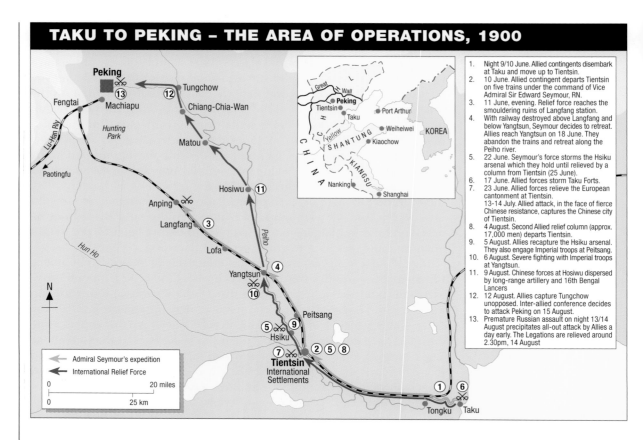

1. Night 9/10 June. Allied contingents disembark at Taku and move up to Tientsin.
2. 10 June. Allied contingent departs Tientsin on five trains under the command of Vice Admiral Sir Edward Seymour, RN.
3. 11 June, evening. Relief force reaches the smouldering ruins of Langfang station.
4. With railway destroyed above Langfang and below Yangtsun, Seymour decides to retreat. Allies reach Yangtsun on 18 June. They abandon the trains and retreat along the Peiho river.
5. 22 June. Seymour's force storms the Hsiku arsenal which they hold until relieved by a column from Tientsin (25 June).
6. 17 June. Allied forces storm Taku Forts.
7. 23 June. Allied forces relieve the European cantonment at Tientsin. 13-14 July. Allied attack, in the face of fierce Chinese resistance, captures the Chinese city of Tientsin.
8. 4 August. Second Allied relief column (approx. 17,000 men) departs Tientsin.
9. 5 August. Allies recapture the Hsiku arsenal. They also engage Imperial troops at Peitsang.
10. 6 August. Severe fighting with Imperial troops at Yangtsun.
11. 9 August. Chinese forces at Hosiwu dispersed by long-range artillery and 16th Bengal Lancers
12. 12 August. Allies capture Tungchow unopposed. Inter-allied conference decides to attack Peking on 15 August.
13. Premature Russian assault on night 13/14 August precipitates all-out attack by Allies a day early. The Legations are relieved around 2.30pm, 14 August

order was immediately reversed. However, an anti-Boxer general, Nieh Shih-ch'eng, was deployed along the railway to stop further Boxer activity and on 6 June, 480 poorly armed Boxers were killed near Langfang. The Governor-General, Yulu, urged the Tsungli Yamen to issue orders to Nieh and other Qing commanders to put down the Boxer movement. By now, however, the attitude of the government had changed markedly, possibly due to the request by foreign ministers to bring up guards from the coast for protection, and no further action was taken against the Boxers.

In the meantime, news of the various outrages had travelled fast forcing many Christian converts to flee towards the capital. Yet the ministers in Peking failed to react as none of their nationals had been killed in this recent outrage. It was in fact a letter sent to the French minister, M. Pichon, from Bishop Favier in Peking which caused the most concern. In it, Favier described the massacres of his fellow Catholics and the pressure that refugees were now placing on the schools and hospitals of Peking. More disconcerting was his assessment that the same could happen to the foreigners in Peking.

Pichon took the gloomy report to his fellow ministers, who dismissed it as nothing more than an overreaction on the part of the Bishop. Their only action was to seek assurances from the government that their lives and property would be safe in the hands of the Chinese authorities. Anything stronger such as calling on reinforcements from the coast or issuing ultimatums was viewed as unnecessary, and it was considered that such actions might create political problems for the government. Sir Claude MacDonald, the British minister, received reassurances from

Prince Ch'ing that no further outrages would be committed by the Boxers and several decrees were issued condemning their activities. Unfortunately for the foreigners, Ch'ing's days as head of the Tsungli Yamen were numbered, and he was replaced on 10 June by Prince Tuan.

Attacks and riots by the Boxers were increasing dramatically. Foreign engineers building the railway to the capital were attacked at Paotingfu on 28 May, the track damaged, and the telegraph destroyed. The engineers and their families fled towards the Yangtse River but were attacked when their boats ran aground and a number were killed. A few days later, two British missionaries were murdered at Yung Ch'ing. When news of these and other atrocities broke in the foreign capitals, revenge became the watchword, and naval forces were moved towards Taku; troops were landed to protect the foreign settlements of Tientsin and Peking. The ministers in the capital gave the government a deadline to quell the Boxers or steps would be taken. When news of further outrages reached Peking including the destruction of the station and trains at Fengtai, there was consternation in the capital. The *Shanghai Mercury* described the situation: 'Immense crowds assembled at the stations and in the streets, eagerly discussing the ever-changing reports that came from a multitude of sources. Excitement ran high and there was a general feeling of alarm.' Fearing for the safety of the foreign community, the ministers applied to the Tsungli Yamen for permission to land forces and bring them up from the coast. On 31 May the *Mercury* reported that 'on Thursday, however, the Chinese officials, finding further resistance useless, granted permission for 30 men of each nationality to go by train and station themselves at their respective Legations, and at 4 o'clock a special train conveyed them to Peking. The "30" men of each nationality were made up as follows: 75 British, 75 Russians, 75 French, 52 Americans, 30 Italians and 30 Japanese, while guards of like strength were left at Tientsin.' Private Oscar Upham of the United States Marine Corps wrote in his diary on the 31st, 'We arrived at the railroad terminus at Peking at about 6pm, then came a forced march of seven miles in heavy marching order to the Legation grounds. At the first gate Captain McCalla thought the Chinese would try to close the gates to keep us out. He gave us double time for about 300 yards. Taking the place with a grandstand rush we kept up a rapid march until we reached the American Legation. We had a good supper awaiting us; we established our post for the night and turned in'. A few days later some more foreign troops arrived. They were to be the last until the middle of August.

A strange silence descended on Peking in those first hot days of June 1900 and a strong sense of expectation prevailed in the Legation Quarter. The day when the Boxers had promised to slaughter all foreigners in the capital, 27 May, had come and gone but even to the most naïve it was clear the threat had not abated and their worst fears might yet come to pass. Some made attempts to flee the capital only to have their hopes dashed. 'We went to the railroad,' wrote one American lady, 'and in company with a number of missionaries waited from ten o'clock until five in the evening for a train to take us to Tientsin, but the last one had gone the day before [June 4] at 3.20pm. We went back to the Legation and prepared for the worst. On the way we were surrounded by a howling mob of Chinese. We made our way with much difficulty, although none of the Chinese offered us bodily harm. It was not long thereafter before the serious trouble began.'

CHRONOLOGY

1839–1842 First China War (Opium War)
1858–1860 Second China War

1860
13 Oct Entry of allies into Peking

1894–1895 Sino-Japanese War

1898 Dowager Empress usurps the throne in a coup d'état. Five reformers are beheaded

1899
18 Oct. Pitched battle between Boxers and General Yuan's Imperial troops
26 Dec. Yüan Shih k'ai appointed Governor of Shantung Province

1900
28 May Boxers attack station and rolling stock at Fengtai
30 May Allied fleet begins to assemble off Taku Bar in the Gulf of Pechili. Allied marines arrive at Tongku and Tientsin
31 May Allied marines and sailors arrive at Peking Legations
3 June Arrival of German and Austrian Guards in Peking.
6 June Railway from Peking to Tientsin destroyed by Boxers
8 June State of semi-siege in Peking
Prince Tuan appointed President of the Tsungli Yamen
9 June Peking Race Course destroyed by Boxers. Sir Claude MacDonald wires Admiral Seymour to send troops
10 June Telegraph line from Peking destroyed by Boxers. Seymour expedition sets out from Tientsin
11 June Murder of Chancellor Sugiyama Akira near the Yung Ting Men, Peking. Seymour expedition reached Langfang
13 June Burning of foreign premises in Peking
14 June Burning of foreign premises in Tientsin
15 June Boxer attacks at Tientsin
16 June Over 4,000 stores and the Ch'ien Men destroyed by fire in Peking
17 June Foreign Concession at Tientsin shelled and besieged by Boxers
Attack on the Taku Forts
1.00am Allied boats commence bombardment of Taku Forts
3.00am Allied troops landed on mud flats near Northwest Fort
5.00am Light aids allied accuracy and two magazines blow up
6.00am Allied troops charge Northwest Fort and capture it by storm
6.05am Large explosion at South Fort
6.10am Allied troops take North Fort
6.15am South Fort and Southwest Fort run up white flags
19 June Ultimatum for all foreigners to leave Peking by the Tsungli Yamen. Seymour expedition retreats from Yangtsun

20 June	**Siege of the Foreign Legations begins**
	Baron Klemens von Ketteler, German Minister, murdered. Flight of foreigners to British Legation
4.00pm	Legation Quarter of Peking besieged. Roman Catholic Mission at Peitang Cathedral, Peking, besieged
22 June	Capture of Hsiku Arsenal
23 June	Allied Relief Column enters Tientsin ending first siege. Burning of Hanlin College, Peking
25 June	Seymour expedition relieved
26 June	Seymour expedition returns to Tientsin
30 June–1 July	
	Massacre of missionaries and converts at Paotingfu
3 July	Capture of Chinese position on Peking City Wall
9 July	Allies capture west arsenal at Tientsin
13 July	Allied troops attack the walled city of Tientsin
14 July	Allied troops capture the walled city of Tientsin
17 July	Truce at Legation Quarter, Peking
18 July	Mine explosion at the Peitang Cathedral
25 July	Firing resumes in Peking for a few days
4 August	2.30pm Allied Relief Expedition leaves Tientsin for Peking; bivouac at Hsiku
5 August	Allies capture Hsiku Arsenal and Peitsang; bivouac at Tao-Wa-She
6 August	Capture of Yangtsun; bivouac at Yangtsun
7 August	Bivouac at Yangtsun
8 August	Relief force departs Yangtsun at 5 am; bivouac at Tsaitsun
9 August	Depart at 7.30am; brief battle at Hosiwu; bivouac at Peh-Meaou
10 August	Late departure from Hosiwu due to extreme exhaustion of troops; bivouac at Tsun-ping and Matou
11 August	Entire day in bivouac at Matou; departure at 5.30pm; bivouac at Chang-chai-wan
12 August	Advance to Tungchow, which is captured; bivouac at Tungchow. Mine explosion at the Peitang Cathedral
13 August	Another mine explosion at the Peitang Cathedral. Reconnaissance of Peking; some troops bivouac at Tungchow; others advance to Kai-Pei-Tien
14 August	Relief of Peking
	Siege of Foreign Legations ends
15 August	Empress and courtiers quit Peking northwards. Allies capture Imperial City
16 August	Peitang Cathedral relieved
28 August	Allied victory parade in Forbidden City
3 Sept	Prince Ch'ing returns to Peking
8 Sept	Punitive Expedition departs for Tiu-Liu
10 Sept	Punitive Expedition departs for Liang-hsian
16 Sept	Punitive Expedition departs for Pa-ta-chal
25 Sept	Punitive Expedition departs for Nam-Hing-Men. Field Marshal Count Alfred von Waldersee arrives at Taku
12 Oct	Punitive Expedition departs for Paotingfu
26 Oct	Empress arrives at Sian (Xian)
6 Nov	Punitive Expedition departs for Kalgan
31 Dec	Public execution of von Kettler's confessed murderer
1901	
1 Jan	Parade of Allied troops in Peking
7 Sept	Peace Protocol signed by China and the Allies

OPPOSING COMMANDERS

While there were no identifiable Chinese leaders involved directly in the siege of the Legations, the Boxers and the Imperial soldiers were encouraged by Tzu Hsi (Cixi), the Empress Dowager and her cohort, Prince Tuan. Within the besieged compounds, the small band of defenders was 'led' by Sir Claude MacDonald, the British Minister in Peking, who assumed the duties of Commander-in-Chief during the siege. The first allied expeditionary force that set out for Peking was under the direction of Admiral Sir Edward Seymour; the subsequent relieving force was commanded by General Sir Alfred Gaselee, while Count von Waldersee assumed command of the allied occupation forces.

Tzu Hsi, the Empress Dowager

While the Boxers had no clear leader, much of the blame for the siege of the Peking Legations was placed squarely at the feet of the Empress Dowager, Tzu Hsi. Her origins were simple and although born of a noble Manchu family, she was sold into slavery as a result of her family's poverty. However, her beauty attracted the Emperor Hsien-Feng who made her one of his favourite concubines in 1850. The result of their union, Tung Chih, was named the heir to the throne. Tzu Hsi was a schemer and manipulator with a natural talent for intrigue and she was able to develop strong support in the palace. With the emperor's death in 1861, some say by poison, Tzu Hsi assumed the role of regent until her son achieved his majority in 1874. Afflicted with poor health, the young emperor ruled for only three years before he too succumbed. Once again power shifted back to the Empress, who now acted as regent for her nephew, Kuang Hsü. Although he was to assume the position of emperor in 1889, the real power remained with the Empress, who virtually banished the young emperor from Peking. Indeed following a coup d'état in 1898, the Emperor's powers were stripped away, and this resulted in a period of reaction which culminated in the Boxer Rebellion. While Tzu Hsi did not actually foster the anti-foreign movement, she at least turned a blind eye to its growth, and her complicity in the later phases of the rebellion is indisputable.

During the siege of the Legations, she issued a stream of edicts denouncing the foreign presence, but much of the army's strategy was guided by Prince Tuan. With the final capitulation of Chinese forces in Peking, the Empress and her court were forced to quit the capital on 15 August 1900 and settle at Sian in Shensi Province where she was the de facto ruler of the country, finally returning to the capital on 6 January 1902. Tzu Hsi was to rule China for another six years until her death on 15 November 1908.

A Chinese portrait of the 'Empress Mother' Tzu Hsi, the Empress Dowager, from a plate published in *Harper's Magazine* in September 1899. The Empress was an enigma to the allies for on the one hand she openly encouraged the Boxers whilst showing restraint against the besieged Legations. She was a ruthless leader of China who thought nothing of destroying anyone who stood in her way and in her final ten years of life her authority was not seriously challenged. (Anne S.K. Brown Military Collection, Brown University Library)

Prince Tuan

Born as Tsai I, Prince Tuan (Duan) inherited his rank in 1860 but spent the next thirty years in the political wilderness. However, in 1898 he emerged from isolation with other conservatives to defend the Empress Dowager, whose position was threatened. He was mainly responsible for purging the reformers, many of whom were beheaded. The Empress took kindly to his work and he became a court favourite no doubt helped by his connections to the royal family through marriage. Tuan's own son, P'un Chun, was chosen to succeed the emperor, Kuang Hsü, who was faltering as ruler. This change in succession was viewed with considerable opposition by the foreign powers, who feared anti-foreign uprisings. There was also internal opposition to Tuan's manipulations and Kuang Hsü managed to hold on to his power. Tuan, seeing this as a result of foreign pressure, became more xenophobic and threw in his lot with the Boxers.

By June 1900 Tuan had manoeuvred himself into a position of considerable power and influence in the court and his scheming led to a shake-up in the Tsungli Yamen, the Chinese Foreign Office, with the removal of the moderate Prince Ch'ing (Qing) and others on 10 June. Tuan himself now assumed control of this important office. It was this development which struck fear into the foreign residents in Peking and led to the organisation of defences in anticipation of anti-foreign riots. Throughout the duration of the siege Prince Tuan was the loudest critic of the foreigners, and commanded the 10,000 Boxers who assaulted the Peitang Cathedral for almost two months. Following the relief of the capital, a decree was issued naming him as one of the co-conspirators of the Boxers and removing him from office. While many no doubt urged his execution he along with his brother were banished for life to Xinjiang in the far north west of the country.

Sir Claude Maxwell MacDonald

The son of an army officer, MacDonald was born in 1852 and like many of his class received military training at Sandhurst and subsequently joined the 74th Highlanders at the age of 20. He attained the rank of major in 1882, the same year that he saw action in the campaign against the Egyptians. Two years later he was serving in the Suakin campaign with the 42nd Highlanders and was wounded at the battle of Tamai, and although he was still in the army spent the next several years in consular and government positions in various parts of Africa where he displayed remarkable administrative and diplomatic qualities.

Following his retirement from the military in 1896, MacDonald was appointed to the position of British minister in Peking and his successes included the leases on Weihaiwei and the extension on Hong Kong, and the opening of various Chinese rivers to western trade and navigation. He was made a Knight Commander of the Order of the Bath in 1898.

His military experience made him the obvious choice to assume overall command of the defence of the Legations, and he was notably one of the few ministers in Peking to take an active part in the defence. Polly Condit Smith, one of the besieged, noted in her diary that he tried to do his duty but had difficulty giving orders to other nationals who envied his position and that of the British Legation. Nonetheless, he was able to maintain cohesion among the foreign nationals to the point

A contemporary photograph of Sir Claude MacDonald. A note in the *Graphic* summed up his efforts: 'When the storm actually burst, Sir Claude, being a born soldier, showed at his best, and it may well be questioned whether the Legations would have survived but for his capable leadership. By unanimous consent he took command of the strangely assorted international assemblage of military and civilians.' (Anne S.K. Brown Military Collection, Brown University Library)

Admiral Sir Edward Seymour, who commanded the first relief expedition. He was described as a 'man of a singularly broad and humane outlook, with a particular capacity for appreciating the point of view of others; this contributed largely to the harmony of his relations with foreign officers serving under him'. (Anne S.K. Brown Military Collection, Brown University Library)

where they were able to withstand various onslaughts from the Chinese until Peking was relieved in August 1900. For his efforts, he was promoted a Knight Grand Cross of the Order of St. Michael and St. George in 1901 and received the military KCB in the same year. The next four years were spent as the British consul in Toyko becoming Britain's first ambassador to Japan in 1905. He negotiated the Anglo-Japanese naval treaty of 1905, retired in 1912 and died three years later in London.

Much of the credit for withstanding the fifty-five-day siege can be attributed directly to MacDonald's tireless leadership. To create a defence force out of a ragtag body of soldiers and civilians and organise various committees to administer the day-to-day needs of the foreign community in Peking was no mean feat and MacDonald was the right man for the task. It is doubtful if the Legations would have survived but for his capable command. Someone remarked that 'he brought the same quiet resource, diligence and wholeheartedness to the task before him', but that he underrated the seriousness of the situation until too late; and that he failed like many others to quite 'grasp the subtleties of Chinese character, and to foresee an impending crisis'.

Admiral Sir Edward Seymour

The British admiral who would lead the first unsuccessful attempt to relieve the Peking Legations began his naval career as a midshipman on board HMS *Terrible* during the Crimean War in the Black Sea, being present at the bombardment of Odessa and Sebastopol. During the China War of 1857 he was on a launch from HMS *Calcutta* when the launch was sunk during the destruction of the Chinese flotilla at Fatsha Creek. Promoted sub-lieutenant in the same year, he achieved the rank of lieutenant in 1860. Seymour was severely wounded during an incident in the Congo River in 1870 when, as commander of the *Growler*, he rescued a British vessel from pirates. Twelve years later saw him in command of the *Iris* during the Egyptian revolt, and several years later he was promoted aide-de-camp to Queen Victoria. He was second-in-command of the Channel Squadron from 1892 until 1894.

Seymour was appointed to the post of commander-in-chief of the China Station in December 1897 in which capacity he was serving when he received news from Sir Claude MacDonald of the situation in Peking. The allied fleet which assembled in the Gulf of Pechihli off Taku Bar, consisting of 36 vessels from several nations, was placed under the overall command of Seymour, the senior naval commander, and it was his decision to land troops and send a relief expedition to the beleaguered city as well as to capture the Taku Forts at the mouth of the Peiho River. While the latter was successful, his expedition to relieve the Legations failed in the face of strong Chinese resistance at various places along the railway line to Peking.

The first decade of the twentieth century saw Seymour travelling to a number of foreign capitals in the company of various high-ranking British dignitaries. He retired from the navy in 1910 and died in Berkshire in 1929.

Seymour's expeditionary force was notable in the annals of military history because it was one of the first multinational forces of the modern era. While it met with limited success, it proved that troops from different nations could fight together in spite of the language barriers

Brigadier-General Sir Alfred Gaselee in command of the British forces sent from India in 1900, photographed by Bassano and published in July 1900. He was 56 years old in 1900 and had seen action in many campaigns in India. Due to the delay in the arrival of Count von Waldersee, Gaselee found himself in command of the allied relief operation against Peking in August 1900. (Anne S.K. Brown Military Collection, Brown University Library)

Field Marshal Count von Waldersee was appointed Commander-in-Chief of the Allied Forces in China in August 1900 although he did not arrive in the country until the following month. Due to the murder of von Ketteler, Germany was given the leading role in the relief expedition and supplied the commander. Unfortunately, once he arrived, he rapidly became unpopular as a result in particular of his liaison with a young Chinese girl whom he had met previously in Berlin. (Anne S.K. Brown Military Collection, Brown University Library)

and organisational difficulties. The admiral displayed gallantry and tact throughout the expedition, and Captain McCalla, senior officer of the United States contingent, remarked that during the almost continuous engagements, Seymour was 'constantly with the advance guard, and so freely exposed himself that both his own officers and mine feared lest we should be deprived of his conspicuous skill in directing movements …' Another colleague and friend, Flag Lieutenant Frederick A. Powlett, wrote in a letter of 27 June 1900 that 'Edward has behaved absolutely disgracefully, exposed himself recklessly, led most of the charges and generally been most naughty. The men are awfully pleased, naturally, but it is not right, his life is too valuable.'

General Sir Alfred Gaselee

Born in Essex in 1844, Gaselee became a cadet at the Royal Military College, Sandhurst, in 1861, receiving a commission in the 93rd Infantry Regiment two years later. His first experience of combat took place the same year on India's turbulent North-West Frontier. His next campaign was in Abyssinia in 1867 where he served with an Indian regiment and was present at the storming of Magdala in April 1868. Gaselee spent the next twenty years in India and Afghanistan serving in the Second Afghan War of 1878–80 where he accompanied Sir Frederick Roberts on the march from Kabul to Kandahar in 1880, with the Zhob Field Force in 1884, and commanded a brigade during the Tirah campaign of 1897–98.

When the Boxer revolt broke out in 1900 Sir Alfred was appointed to command the British expeditionary force, which was part of the allied relief force under the overall command of the German Count Alfred von Waldersee. Gaselee arrived in Tientsin on 27 July 1900 and was the senior officer then in China. Waldersee's arrival was delayed and command of the relief force fell to Gaselee. He was decisive and firm in the face of inter-allied feuding and countless delays, and it was his column which entered Peking on 14 August 1900. For his services he was promoted major-general, becoming a full general in 1906. He returned to India following the rebellion and finished his military career there in 1909; he died in Surrey in March 1918. Gaselee was described as being 'possessed of sound judgement … absolutely straightforward, he inspired confidence in all who served under him'.

Count Alfred von Waldersee

Born in 1832, von Waldersee served in the war against Austria in 1866 with the Prussian artillery, and four years later as aide-de-camp to King William in the war against France, seeing action at Gravelotte, Beamont, Metz and Sedan. Prior to the Franco-Prussian War he had been the Prussian military attaché in Paris, and when German troops arrived on the outskirts of the French capital his knowledge was of the utmost importance. During this war as one writer described it, 'he displayed conspicuous tact in executing several delicate missions', and following the end of hostilities he became the German Chargé d'Affaires in Paris. Later he commanded the 9th Army Corps, served as an army inspector, and succeeded von Moltke as chief of the general staff. He was promoted to the rank of Field Marshal when the Crown Prince came of age.

When the rebellion broke out in 1900 and allied forces began to concentrate off China, he was appointed to command them although he had not yet arrived in the country. In fact the first phase of the campaign – the capture of the Taku Forts and the relief of Tientsin and Peking – were all conducted without his presence. Von Waldersee did not arrive in Tientsin until 27 September 1900 and it was only from this date onward that he played a significant part in events. This consisted largely of the direction of the various punitive expeditions. With a strong desire to avenge the murder of Count von Ketteler in June 1900 as the impetus, Germany took the lead in the prosecution of these expeditions. Von Waldersee, with the blessing of Kaiser Wilhelm, carried out a vicious campaign to crush any further Boxer opposition killing many innocent Chinese in the process. On 2 February 1901 von Waldersee presided over a parade through Peking of representatives of all the allied contingents. He became a legendary figure in Chinese novels and historical fiction as a result of his liaison with a young and attractive Chinese girl whom he had met earlier in Berlin, despite being married to the American widow of Prince Frederick of Schleswig-Holstein.

OPPOSING FORCES

The siege involved a ragtag defence 'force' of foreign nationals from eight nations supplemented by a small number of regular soldiers, sailors and marines, and assisted by Chinese Christian converts, arrayed against a besieging force initially made up of members of the secret society known as the 'Boxers'. Later, the bulk of the besieging force was made up of elements of the Imperial Chinese Army. Similarly, the Imperial army constituted the chief threat to the various relief expeditions involving troops from Britain and her Indian colonies, and soldiers, sailors and marines from the United States, Germany, Japan, Austria, France, Russia and Italy.

CHINESE FORCES

The Boxers

The Boxers grew out of the popular culture of North China and developed from various different secret societies composed mainly of young Chinese males. What they lacked in leadership they made up for with a fanatical zeal in their desire to rid China of all foreigners and to replace the ruling Manchus, who they viewed as foreign usurpers. As the movement expanded, new groups identified themselves with one or another Chinese trigram (an inscription or character of three strokes or letters), the most common being the *kan* and *qian* trigrams. They imitated the dress of martial arts performers but they distinguished themselves from the masses by wearing special items of clothing. The *kan* trigram wore red caps or turbans, a red sash or scarf, and red leggings or ankle strap; the *qian* trigram Boxers preferred yellow. A village would have a single Boxer unit (or *tuan*) of anywhere from 25 to 100 men, with larger settlements having more units. Each unit was led by a Senior Brother-Disciple (*da shixiong*), chosen often because of his superior boxing skills. The rest of the unit were called Brother-Disciples (*shixiong*). There was a distinction between military (*wu*) units and civil (*wen*) units, the latter being composed mainly of educated persons. The Red Lanterns (*Hongdengzhao*) were female Boxers dressed entirely in red and were found mostly in the area around Tientsin.

A Boxer 'Standard Bearer' posed with spear and wicker shield, from a photograph by the Royal Engineers. This picture was obviously posed after the siege as a souvenir photograph for the allied troops. The Boxers wore no real uniform but were identified by a piece of red cloth worn somewhere on their body either as a turban, sash or apron. (Jean S. and Frederic A. Sharf Collection)

Chinese troops in a drawing by the German artist Richard Knötel and reproduced in the Leipzig *Illustrierte Zeitung*. On the left are two infantrymen of the Imperial army, while next to them is a drum major of the regular army. Seated on a trunk is a field artilleryman while the figure in the foreground on the right is a Boxer. (Anne S.K. Brown Military Collection, Brown University Library)

At the beginning the Boxers were armed with primitive weapons including long swords and knives, and ancient firearms. Each new recruit had to undergo an initiation rite involving the learning of incantations. Once he reached the stage of being 'under the spell', he was regarded as being immune to bullets, usually demonstrated to the uninitiated by firing blank bullets at his body. These demonstrations often took place at boxing grounds established throughout the country.

The Chinese Imperial Army

The humiliation of the defeat by Japan in the Korean war of 1894–95 led to some reform of the Chinese army by the time of the Boxer rebellion. A mere three-fifths of those Chinese troops mobilised for the 1894 war had been armed with any kind of rifle, the majority carrying only pikes, swords or spears. Although there were nine arsenals or machine shops by 1894, the Chinese were still producing old muskets and gingals alongside newer firearms. As a result of the war new military units were formed by Jung-Lu, President of the Board of War, modelled on the western style. These were the 'Self-strengthening Army' under Chang Chih-tung, and the 'Pacification Army' (or 'Newly Created') commanded after December 1895 by Yüan Shi-k'ai. The Self-strengthening Army had eight battalions of infantry, two squadrons of cavalry, two brigades of artillery, and one company of engineers. It resembled a German-style brigade and employed German officers to train the men. This army became the model for the new-style armies in the southern part of the country. The Pacification Army was composed of two 'wings' of two and three battalions respectively, artillery, a reserve unit and four troops of cavalry; services included bridging, fortifications, mine-laying, ordnance repair and telegraph detachments. These two armies were the only western-modelled military units available to the Chinese at the time of the Boxer rebellion, but saw no action as their commanders actively avoided confrontation with the foreign troops.

In addition there was the 'Tenacious Army' of 30 battalions under Nieh Shih-ch'eng and also modelled on German standards, the 'Resolute Army' under Sung Ch'ing, and the 'Kansu Braves' under Tung Fu-hsiang. The strength of the former was around 10,000 men divided into eight battalions of infantry, two squadrons of cavalry, two brigades of artillery, and one company of engineers. It along with the Pacification Army were the only two Chinese armies that had really evolved from backward militia armies. A militia organisation of reservists, the Green Standard and the Bannermen, was maintained also.

In September 1898, Jung-Lu was given sole command of these armies and organised the Tenacious, the Kansu Irregulars, the Self-strengthening and the Pacification armies into four divisions, the Left, Right, Front and Rear, to form an army corps known as the Guards Army. The Front Division made up from the old Tenacious Army consisted of around 13,000 men and was stationed near Tientsin. It was well armed with Mauser rifles, Maxim machine guns, and a variety of artillery pieces. Next came the Left Division drawn from the old Resolute Army and numbering around 10,000 men with weapons similar to the Front Division. The Kansu Braves or Irregulars now became the Rear Division. Mostly made up of Muslims, it had around 10,000 poorly armed and ill-disciplined troops. Making up the Right Division were the troops of the Pacification or Newly Created Army, considered to be the best organized of the Guards Army. An additional centre division under the direct command of Jung-Lu himself was made up almost entirely of Manchu Bannermen and numbered under 10,000 men, located south of the capital. A further 30,000 troops in the Peiyang area were to be strictly drilled.

The five divisions consisted of eight battalions made up of five infantry, one cavalry, one artillery and one engineer battalion each. A training battalion was attached to the divisions. On paper four companies of 250 men made up each battalion but this was rarely the case except in a few of the divisions. A British naval observer who visited China in 1898 commented that few of the Chinese troops had achieved anything resembling western military standards and on the whole were poorly equipped.

The Guards Army, sometimes referred to as the Grand Army of the North, was intended to defend the capital and the Empress Dowager. Prince Tuan and other leaders openly sided with the Boxers and as sympathy for the Boxer cause grew, soldiers from the Guards Army began to fight against the allies. Most of the siege operations against the Peking Legations were conducted by troops under the command of Jung-Lu.

Estimates of the actual number of troops available to China on the eve of the rebellion vary. One figure puts the number of Disciplined Forces around 360,000, while another, including Green Standard and Bannermen militia estimates around 1,752,000. However, only a small fraction were actually mobilised and fought against the allies. In the early weeks of the Boxer Rebellion, the Chinese Imperial Army stayed neutral and in some cases even fought the Boxers, as General Yüan Shi-k'ai's troops did in northern Shantung Province. As late as 15 June 1900, the Imperial soldiers had not raised arms against the foreigners but within two days were attacking contingents of the allied relief force at Yangtsun.

ORDER OF BATTLE

CHINESE IMPERIAL ARMY

Commander-in-Chief: Jung-Lu
STRENGTH: estimate 1,700,000 men

1. GUARDS ARMY (30-40,000 men)

Left Division (Resolute Army) (General Sung Ch'ing)
Right Division (Pacification or Newly Created Army) (General Yüan Shih-k'ai)
Front Division (Tenacious Army) (General Nieh Shih-ch'eng)
Rear Division (Kansu Irregulars) (General Tung Fu-hsiang)
Centre Division (Manchu Bannermen) (General Jung-Lu)

2. Self-strengthening Army (transferred to Woosung 1896)

3. MILITIA, RESERVISTS AND POLICE

Bannermen
Green Standard

ALLIED FORCES

The Besieged

The military forces available to Sir Claude MacDonald in Peking during the period from the end of May 1900 until 14 August consisted of little

A company of Chinese troops marching down a Peking street after a photograph by L.R. Barr, a student interpreter at the British Legation, and published in the *Illustrated London News*. They carry their rifles over their shoulders holding them by the muzzle. The Chinese enlisted man, in baggy trousers and a brightly coloured, ill-fitting jacket, topped by a turban or a conical bamboo hat, was in striking contrast to the comparatively subdued appearance of troops of the allied armies. (Anne S.K. Brown Military Collection, Brown University Library)

Sir Claude MacDonald seated with the Customs Volunteers men in a photograph taken by the Revd C.A. Killie after the siege. These volunteers came from the Chinese Maritime Customs and were active in the defence of the Legation Quarter during the siege. One British soldier arriving in Peking following the relief noted that 'civilians were strutting about armed to the teeth, with their rifles, bandoleers, etc., all day long'. (Jean S. and Frederic A. Sharf Collection)

more than 400 marine guards from the eight countries of Austria-Hungary, France, Germany, Great Britain, Italy, Japan, Russia and the United States. Some of these troops, referred to as the 'Winter Guard', had arrived in late May 1900 at the request of the foreign consuls. Private Oscar Upham of the United States Marines Corps described the movement on 31 May: ' … in the meantime we bulldozed the officials into letting us have a train which was made up of one gondola for baggage, ammunition and guns, and ten coaches for the troops, which were made up of Americans, English, Russians, Japanese, Italians, Austrians and French. We arrived at the railroad terminus at Peking at about 6 pm, then came a forced march of seven miles in heavy marching order to the Legation grounds.' Besides rifles and handguns, the only major armaments available was an Austrian Maxim gun, a British Nordenfeldt gun, a 1-pdr quick-firing gun supplied by the Italian contingent and an American Colt machine gun. Later a makeshift gun called the 'International' or 'Betsy' was assembled from an old cannon found in a junk shop.

Russian Marines in Tientsin, 1900. Russia was the weak link in the allied forces in China even though she supplied the second largest contingent after Japan, and during the assault on Peking in August 1900, the Russians' premature advance against the wrong target caused initial confusion among the other allied troops. They were indiscriminate in their treatment of the Chinese and were notable for their looting of Chinese palaces in Peking. (Peabody Essex Institute, Salem, MA)

Supplementing the meagre professional force manning the barricades and defences were the volunteers – civilians pressed into duty as soldiers. For the majority, their only taste of the military, as one observer cynically quipped, was observing a parade in London. One group of 75 men was known as Thornhill's Roughs emulating the Rough Riders of San Juan Hill fame, but in reality little more than a 'carving knife brigade' from the weapons they wielded. Another group were the Customs Volunteers – men from the Chinese Maritime Customs who played an important role in the defence of the Legation Quarter.

It was a similar situation in Tientsin, where after Seymour had departed a small number of trained soldiers and sailors served alongside volunteer groups in the defence of the place, although 1,700 Russians with cavalry and field guns reached the city on 13 June.

The Allied Fleet

On 1 June 1900 Admiral Sir Edward Seymour wrote from his ship off Taku Bar, 12 miles offshore, to Sir Claude MacDonald in Peking that 'there are 17 men of war of sorts here now'. This fleet would swell over the coming months as other ships arrived. The vessels from eight allied nations included the British ships *Alacrity, Algerine, Aurora, Barfleur, Centurion, Endymion, Fame, Whiting*, and *Orlando* drawn from Her Britannic Majesty's Squadron in China and Japan under Admiral Sir Edward Seymour; from the *Division Navale Française de L'Extreme Orient et du Pacifique Occidental* commanded by Contre-Admiral C.L.C. Courrejolles were several ships including the *Lion*; the Russian Pacific Naval Squadron commanded by Vice-Admiral Hiltebrandt included the *Rossia, Korietz, Bobr, Silatch,* and *Gilyak*; some of these vessels were later to see action in the war against Japan in 1904. From the United States Naval Squadron, Asiatic Station, under the command of Rear-Admiral Louis Kempff, came the *Monocacy* which arrived in May, and the *Nashville* and

Newark which arrived in June. The Imperial German Navy, Pacific, commanded by Vice-Admiral Bendemann included the *Kaiserin-Augusta, Hertha, Hansa, Irene, Gefion, Jaguar* and *Iltis*; while the Imperial Japanese Navy was represented by *Atago, Kasagi* and *Kagero*. There were also vessels from the Italian and Austrian navies. The majority of Admiral Seymour's force in the first relief column were drawn from these ships.

Those ships directly involved in the bombardment of the Taku Forts on 17 June 1900 were the dispatch vessel *Alacrity* (Commander A.H. Smith-Dorien), the sloop *Algerine* (Commander E.J.W. Slade), the *Atago* (Commander H. Jakenouchi), the gunboat *Bobr* (Commander Dobrovolsky), the torpedo-boat destroyer *Fame* (Lieutenant Commander R.J.B. Keyes), the *Gilyak* (Commander Larionoff), the gunboat *Iltis* (Commander Lans), the gunboat *Korietz* (Commander Sillman), the *Lion* (Commandant Amet), the cruiser *Monocacy* (Captain Wise), and the torpedo-boat destroyer *Whiting* (Lieutenant Commander J.E. Kelly).

Chinese soldiers of the Weihaiwei Regiment (1st Chinese Regiment) in ceremonial dress. This photograph was taken at Weihaiwei. The regiment was trained and staffed by British officers and served with distinction during the defence of Tientsin, the relief of Seymour's expedition, and during the assault on Peking. (Jean S. and Frederic A. Sharf Collection)

Admiral Seymour's Relief force

Seymour's force, which left Tientsin in the early hours of Sunday, 10 June 1900, consisted of 2,072 men and 116 officers organised into the International Relief Expedition (these figures vary in different accounts but the usual estimate is just over 2,000 men). Britain supplied 921 sailors and marines; there were 450 Germans, mostly sailors, and 305 Russian sailors; the French sent 158 sailors, the Americans 112 sailors, Austria 25, Italy 40 and Japan 54. Equipment included seven field guns and ten machine guns. The force was carried on five trains with more than 100 railway cars. Train No. 1 contained half the British force, all of the Americans and Austrians in addition to coolies and supplies to repair the track; No. 2 carried the remainder of the British, all of the Japanese and some of the French; No. 3 had only Germans on board; No. 4 carried the Russians, Italians and the remaining French; and No. 5 carried supplies and was supposed to shuttle back and forth between Tientsin.

General Gaselee's Relief Force

As Count von Waldersee was not due to arrive in time, command of the second relief force devolved to General Gaselee. He had at his disposal approximately 18,000 men. As most of the British Army was currently engaged in the war against the Boers in South Africa, the majority of the British contingent of 2,900 men and 12 guns were drawn from India. It was made up of men from the Naval Brigade, 12th Battery Royal Field Artillery, Hong Kong and Singapore Artillery, 2nd Battalion Royal Welch Fusiliers, 1st Bengal Lancers, 7th Rajput Infantry, 24th Punjab Infantry, 1st Sikh Infantry, Hong Kong Regiment, 1st Chinese Regiment, Royal Engineers, signalmen and telegraphists. In terms of combat experience, the Indian troops had seen action in the Chitral and Tirah campaigns of the 1890s.

The American force of 2,200 men and six guns, consisted of 9th Infantry Regiment, 14th Infantry Regiment, one battalion of the United States Marine Corps, Light Battery 'F' 5th Artillery (Reilly's Battery), and one troop of the 6th Cavalry. These troops had been dispatched from the Philippines, where they had been involved in quelling the Filipino insurgents, and prior to that had fought in the war with Spain in 1898. Japan sent by far the largest contingent, 9,000 men in all with 24 guns. They came from the 5th Division, comprising nine battalions of infantry, six batteries of artillery, and four squadrons of cavalry. It had been five years since Japan had been involved in a war but her troops were well trained and adapted to the heat of China.

From Russia came 2,900 men and 16 guns. There were three infantry battalions of the East Siberian Regiment, two batteries of artillery and one squadron of cavalry. Few of these men had seen combat beyond some of the fighting at Tientsin and many were raw conscripts. One thousand two hundred men and 12 guns came from France, made up of two battalions of the *Infanterie de la Marine*, one Naval Battalion, and one artillery battalion. They too, had little combat experience.

ORDER OF BATTLE

ALLIED FORCES

LEGATION QUARTER
Commander-in-Chief: Sir Claude MacDonald
Strength: 543 men

Artillery: Italian 1-pdr. gun (120 rounds); American Colt (25,000 rounds); British five-barrelled Nordenfelt; Austrian machine gun; the 'International' or 'Betsy'

REGULAR TROOPS (392 MEN)
American: 53 Marines, 3 officer (Captains Myers and Hall, Surgeon Lippett)
Austrian: 30 Seamen; 5 officers (Captains Thornton and Kollar, Lieutenant von Winterhalter, Sub-Lieutenant Meyer, Baron Boynberg)
British: 79 Royal Marine Light Infantry, 3 officers (Captains Strouts, Halliday and Wray); 3 seamen;
Visting: Captain Poole, East Yorkshire Regiment; Captain Smith, South Staffs. Regiment (retd.); Captain Oliphant, Scots Greys (retd.)
French: 45 Seamen; 2 officer (Lieutenant Darcy and Midshipman Herbert);
Visting: Captain Labrousse, Marine Infantry
German: 51 Marines (3rd Battalion), 1 officer (Lieutenant Graf von Sodon);
Visting: Lieutenant von Strauch, Imperial Guard (retd.)
Italian: 28 Seamen; 1 officers (Lieutenant Paolini)
Japanese: 24 Marines, 2 officers (Lieutenant Hara); Lt Col Shiba (Military Attaché);
Visting: Captains Morita and Ando

Russian: 72 Seamen; 2 officers (Lieutenants Baron von Rahden and von Dehn); 7 Cossack Legation Guards; *Visting:* Lieutenant Vroublevsky, 9th Eastern Siberian Rifles

Volunteer Force (125 men) (Captain Poole)
Auxiliary:
Customs Volunteers (Lieutenant von Strauch)
British Legation Volunteers (Mr. Russell)
Russian Volunteers (Mr. Wassilieff)
French Volunteers (Mr. Bureau)
Belgian Volunteers
Miscellaneous Volunteers
Thornhill's Rough's (50 men)

PEITANG (OR NORTH) CATHEDRAL
Commander-in-Chief: Bishop Favier
Strength: 43 men

Regular Troops (43 men)
French: 30 seamen, 1 officer (Lieutenant Paul Breton – killed 30 July)
Italian: 11 seamen, 1 officer (Lieutenant Olivieri)

ADMIRAL SEYMOUR'S RELIEF FORCE
Commander-in-Chief: Admiral Sir Edward Seymour
Strength: 2,072 men
Transport: 5 trains

American: (Captain McCalla):
106 sailors and marines (US Navy and Marine Corps)

Austrian:
24 sailors (Imperial Austrian Navy)

British: (Admiral Sir Edward Seymour):
640 sailors (ship's companies from HMS *Endymion* and *Centurion*)
213 marines (Royal Marine Light Infantry – Major J. R. Johnstone)

French:
151 sailors (*Division Navale Française*)

German: (Captain Von Usedom):
427 sailors (ship's companies from SMS *Gefion*, *Hansa*, *Hertha*, *Iltis*, and SM *Kaiserin-Augusta*)

Italian:
38 sailors (Royal Italian Navy)

Japanese: (Commander Gitaro Mori):
52 sailors (company from *Kasagi*)

Russian:
305 sailors (Imperial Russian Navy)

GENERAL GASELEE'S RELIEF FORCE
Commander-in-Chief: Lt General Sir Alfred Gaselee
Strength: circa 18,000 men

American: (Major General Chaffee)
2,200 men and 6 guns
9th Infantry Regiment
14th Infantry Regiment
1 battalion, United States Marine Corps
Light Battery F, 5th Artillery (Reilly's Battery)
1 troop, 6th Cavalry

British: (Lieutenant-General Gaselee)
2,900 men and 12 guns
Naval Brigade
12th Battery Royal Field Artillery
Hong Kong and Singapore Artillery
2nd Battalion Royal Welch Fusiliers
1st Bengal Lancers
1st Indian Brigade comprising:
    7th Rajput Infantry
    24th Punjab Infantry
    1st Sikh Infantry
    Hong Kong Regiment
    1st Chinese Regiment
    Royal Engineers, signalmen, telegraphists

French: (Major-General Frey)
1,200 men and 12 guns
2 battalions of *Infanterie de la Marine*
1 Naval Battalion
1 artillery battalion

Japanese: (Lieutenant-General Yamagutchi)
9,000 men and 24 guns
5th Division comprising:
9 battalions of Infantry
6 batteries of artillery
4 squadrons of cavalry

Russian: (General Lineivitch)
2,900 men and 16 guns
3 infantry battalions of the East Siberian Regiment
2 batteries of artillery
1 squadron of cavalry

'A' Company, United States Marines en route from Manila to China from a drawing in *Harper's Weekly*. A large contingent of American troops were in the Philippines fighting the Filipino Insurgents under Aguinaldo following the defeat of the Spanish in the war of 1898. When the rebellion broke out in China a number of regiments were shipped to Taku. (Anne S.K. Brown Military Collection, Brown University Library)

OPPOSING PLANS

The Boxer rising was not a formally planned military campaign in the traditional sense, but rather a spontaneous rising by a section of Chinese society against the domination of their country by the foreign powers. As such there was little in the way of identifiable planning. Even the actions of the foreign powers were largely reactive and initially focused on little more than the relief of the settlements at Tientsin and Peking. The appeal of the Boxers to the average Chinese peasant in the late 1890s was their declared goal of destroying the foreign presence in their country, preserving the religions and culture of China, restoring the geographical and political integrity of the country from foreign incursions, and to a lesser extent their anti-Manchu stance, who were considered by some to be non-Chinese. By the summer of 1900, many in the Chinese court and government including the Dowager Empress had come to see the Boxers as the instrument for ridding the country of foreigners and foreign domination. Yet only a few months earlier, many Chinese leaders had urged that the Boxers be suppressed for fears of upsetting other nations. This dichotomy reveals the problems facing the Chinese authorities in 1900: on the one hand they wished for nothing else but to banish foreigners from the country, while at the same time not wanting to offend the various powers who had interests in the country. This further explains the considerable restraint displayed by the Chinese in their prosecution of the siege of the Peking Legations, even to the extent of supplying fresh fruit to the beleaguered defenders on several occasions. With little effort the Chinese could easily have overwhelmed the defenders at any time if they had so wished. The fact that they did not suggests that the moderates in the court and the commander of the Imperial troops, Jung Lu, were not aggressively anti-foreign but, in a court dominated by the extremists, were forced to act as though they were.

While the western powers were shocked and outraged at the various atrocities committed against their citizens between 1898 and 1900, few of the nations other than Germany urged armed intervention. However, once the crisis came to a head and the foreign representatives were caught in Peking two aims quickly emerged: to rescue the foreign community in the capital and punish the Chinese for this breach of international law.

Admiral Seymour and staff photographed on board HMS *Centurion*. Left to right: Flag Lieutenant F.A. Powlett, Flag Captain J.R. Jellicoe, who was to achieve fame at the Battle of Jutland in 1916, Admiral Sir E.H. Seymour and his secretary, Fleet-Paymaster, F.C. Alton. Powlett, Alton and Jellicoe accompanied Seymour on his failed mission, and Jellicoe was wounded at Peitang during the retreat. (Jean S. and Frederic A. Sharf Collection)

However, the response of the allied powers enflamed the situation, leaving the Chinese with little option but to declare war.

The siege of the Legations can be seen as falling into two stages. During the first, which lasted only ten days or so, the Boxers were the main enemies, while the Chinese government and the Imperial army kept somewhat neutral and in some areas the army was even used against the Boxers. In the second stage of approximately eight weeks' duration, the government, court, and army became the enemy and the Boxers almost became ineffective bystanders. The defining moment in the crisis and the one which brought about this significant change was the storming of the forts at Taku on 17 June 1900 which was viewed by the Chinese as an act of war. The government responded by stating that 'our country is therefore at war with yours. You must accordingly quit our capital within twenty-four hours accompanied by all your nationals.' As one writer described the consequence of this: 'Exit Boxers – enter the regular Chinese army.' Thereafter, the foreigners, particularly the various relief columns, faced the full force of China's army.

The besieged hung on, acutely aware of what atrocities had been committed against their countrymen. They expected to be massacred at any moment and while their hopes were kept up by rumours of the various relief forces, few thought that they would be saved in time. Under the leadership of Sir Claude MacDonald, the British Minister in Peking, the plan of the besieged was simple – to hang on as long as possible until help arrived. He therefore established committees to organise among other things food supply, medical needs, and the construction of fortifications.

For the two relief columns the task was quite simply to get through to Peking, relieve the Legations and quell any further Boxer insurrections. The premature news that all foreigners in Peking had been massacred provided the pretext for such a move. Seymour's expedition was a response to the fear that the foreigners in Peking would be isolated and attacked. The governments of the various nations gave the go-ahead to their admirals to do whatever they could to save the foreign nationals. The failure of the first relief expedition was due to Admiral Seymour acting independently of his fellow admirals – an impulsive act in response to Sir Claude MacDonald's urgent call for help. By contrast, the second relief force was successful largely because it was a unified multinational force which brought the full weight of available military resources to bear against the Chinese.

Once Peking had been relieved, the plans of the allies changed from one of saving the foreigners in the capital to one of punishing the perpetrators and destroying the Boxer movement while at the same time using the crisis to further each nation's economic and political designs on China.

Opening Moves

The first two weeks of June 1900 witnessed a series of events in Peking which gradually deteriorated particularly after the allies had stormed the Taku Forts on the 17th. Prior to that it had appeared as though the Chinese were toying with the foreigners in Peking and making veiled threats, but they had not taken any action against the diplomats and their families. Boxers had been seen in and around the foreign enclave and anti-foreign placards had appeared, but on the 9th they struck their first blow when a crowd of rioters burnt down the grandstand of the Peking Race Course situated just beyond the southern gates of the city, killing in the process a number of Chinese Christians who had been forced into the building. The foreign community had created its own culture within Peking and racing was a particular favourite with the diplomatic corps. To the Chinese, the Race Course and the popular race days were seen as symbolic of everything that was bad about foreign culture.

The most significant response and the one which escalated the situation was Sir Claude MacDonald's telegram to Sir Edward Seymour at Taku informing him that 'the situation in Peking is hourly become more serious', and requesting that a relief force be dispatched to the capital. While the diplomatic corps was critical of MacDonald's over-reaction, it nonetheless made preparations to accommodate Chinese converts and other refugees in the Legation Quarter while at the same time handing over responsibility of missionary properties to the Chinese government on the condition that it would be held directly responsible for any damage inflicted by the Boxers. Rumours abounded that part of the railway line between Peking and Tientsin had been destroyed by Boxers who were now pouring into Chihli Province from Shantung Province where the first outrages against foreigners had occurred, and much of the countryside around Tientsin and Peking was under their control. Chinese Imperial troops who had been sent to quell them were either withdrawing or actively collaborating with the rebels, whose widespread appeal was their desire to destroy all semblance of foreign presence in China. It was the misfortune of any foreigners to be left out in the countryside and a number of missionaries and converts were murdered at Tungchow, west of the capital.

THE FIRST RELIEF ATTEMPT

Even though the foreigners in Peking itself were still at peace with their Chinese neighbours in the middle of June, MacDonald's plea for help caused the allied commanders at Taku some concern and their subsequent actions led to an escalation of the situation. The allied fleet of 15 advance vessels had taken up anchorage off Taku Bar in the Gulf of Pechihli by late May as a show of strength to warn the Chinese government that any further outrages committed against their nationals would be tantamount to an act of war. A contingent of foreign troops had been landed on 31 May and entrained for Peking at the request of the diplomats as further protection. A few days later, additional troops had been landed and sent to Tientsin, 30 miles from Taku, in the event that the situation deteriorated. The various allied admirals had agreed that if Peking was cut off, they would dispatch a relief force, but it was the arrival of MacDonald's telegram that brought about the next move.

Admiral Sir Edward Seymour, sensing the urgency of his countryman's request, decided to act and ordered his force ashore with the request that contingents from the other nations follow. 'I am landing at once with all available men,' he stated. It was a hasty move with barely any thought of a plan other than to move on Peking. While Seymour was a good sailor, he lacked experience in land warfare and he

was not the ideal person to lead the expedition but there was probably no one else. The allied force, consisting of British, German, French, Russian, American, Japanese, Italian and Austrian sailors and marines, assembled at Tientsin on 10 June. Shortly after, the combined force of just over 2,100 men set off in five trains in the hope of reaching the capital before nightfall. Their main armament was seven field guns and ten machine guns. Between them lay 80 miles of open ground traversed by the single rail track and exposed to Boxers and a large force of foreign-trained Imperial troops under General Nieh Shih-ch'eng who were now in full support of the rebels' cause. Ironically this same Chinese army had only a week earlier won a successful action against the very Boxers they were now united with.

The journey went well for the first few miles and there was little evidence of the Boxers beyond some burnt tracks as Captain-Lieutenant Paul Schlieper of the German Imperial Navy noted in his diary: 'The rebels had set fire to the wooden sleepers after drenching them with petroleum; many were charred, and several still smoking. The discovery warned us to be on our guard, but no further hindrance was met with.' Schlieper reported passing the camps of the Chinese regular troops (at Yangtsun) who barely stirred as the trains passed: 'It did not look as if

German sailors and marines attacking Chinese troops on the railway track during the Seymour Relief Expedition. Germany dispatched 1,126 men of the 3rd Seebataillon along with other units from Tsingtao to participate in the campaign. (Anne S. K. Brown Military Collection, Brown University Library)

ABOVE **The Hsiku Arsenal in a photograph which was widely published during 1900. After crossing the river in small junks, British and German sailors and marines from Seymour's force captured the arsenal, which was garrisoned by Imperial troops, at 10.00am on 23 June 1900 after heavy fighting. The expedition was forced to wait here until a relief force from Tientsin arrived. The arsenal was destroyed by this force on its retreat back to Tientsin. (Anne S. K. Brown Military Collection, Brown University Library)**

RIGHT **Bivouac outside the Hsiku Arsenal – British troops from Tientsin for the relief of Seymour's Column, in a photograph published in September 1900 in *Navy and Army Illustrated*. In the photograph can be seen Indian troops and members of the Weihaiwei (1st Chinese) Regiment wearing straw-brimmed hats. In the background, Russian troops can be seen marching. (Anne S. K. Brown Military Collection, Brown University Library)**

the camps feared the terrible Boxers much, and experience was to show us later pretty clearly that the regulars had secretly made common cause with them.' A broken bridge was repaired and following a bivouac, the force continued on towards Peking on the 11th albeit slowly. The trains were soon halted at Langfang halfway to the capital where the lines had been torn up. Lacking further equipment to repair the track, requests were sent back to Tientsin for further supplies.

Reports were now reaching Seymour that any retreat back to Tientsin would be difficult as Boxers and Imperial troops had now occupied the line between him and the city. At the same time a messenger from the

American Legation in Peking reached Langfang reporting that there was a great sense of expectation in the capital of the arrival of the relief force. The tracks at Langfang would take about three days to repair. A small defensive position was established there called Fort Gefion after the German ship from which the marines came, and on the 14th, it was attacked by several hundred Boxers. On the following day, Seymour dispatched a train to Tientsin but it was forced to return as the tracks had been destroyed.

Unable to advance northwards in safety or retreat south, Seymour decided upon a river route to Peking which would require retreating to Yangtsun and then striking north up the Peiho River. While a German force was left to guard Langfang, the rest of the allied contingent retreated to Yangtsun, where four junks were captured. On 18 June, the Germans at Langfang were attacked by 4,000 Boxers and Chinese regulars but these were repulsed. Langfang was evacuated and the Germans retreated on their train to Yangtsun. Seymour's worst fears were confirmed when the German commander informed him that Chinese Imperial troops had now taken the field against the allies. As soon as the force had taken to the river the empty trains were plundered by the Boxers. Even progress along the river was hampered due to low water levels and it was decided to march along the river banks, leaving the sick and wounded in the junks sailing close alongside. A council of the various commanding officers decided that any further attempt towards Peking was out of the question and that an immediate retreat to Tientsin should begin.

Captain Schlieper described their situation: 'Our advance now proceeded very slowly. The enemy showed wonderful tenacity and had to be pushed back step by step. When one village was cleared a still hotter fire was sure to be opened on us from the next. It was a tough bit of work.' Eventually, on 22 June, a large building which turned out to be the Chinese Imperial Arsenal at Hsiku was attacked and captured. Although only about 6 miles from the foreign settlement at Tientsin, the messengers dispatched by Seymour were all captured. There was nothing else to do but sit and wait for relief to come, which it did on 25 June when a force of 1,000 Russians, Germans and Japanese were able to fight their way through and escort the force back to Tientsin with losses amounting to 62 killed and 232 wounded. As one writer explained, the disastrous relief attempt had not been wholly Seymour's fault but his main mistake was in moving a large, ill-equipped force inland without guarding his line of supply. The fact that his force was attacked sharply on several occasions after 18 June was not of his doing but a result of events which had taken place on the coast at Taku.

THE CAPTURE OF THE TAKU FORTS

Following Seymour's departure for Peking on 9 June, the remaining admirals had decided not to take any additional action for the time being, but as reports came in of increased Boxer activity over the next two weeks, particularly the occupation of the native city at Tientsin, which threatened the foreign settlement in that city, they began to rethink their strategy. There was also a rumour that a major uprising was

BOXER ATTACK ON ADMIRAL SEYMOUR'S RELIEF EXPEDITION AT LOFA,
11 JUNE 1900
That afternoon the lead train was attacked by the Chinese. 'Not more than a couple of hundred, armed with swords, spears, gingals (blunderbusses) and rifles, many of them being quite boys ... there was no sign of fear or hesitation, and these were not fanatical braves, or the trained soldiers of the Empress, but the quiet peace-loving peasantry – the countryside in arms against the foreigner'. C. Bigham.
(Alan & Michael Perry)

set to begin on the 19th and nothing had been heard from Seymour. All this combined to convince the admirals that they should act sooner rather than later to prevent the Boxers overwhelming the foreign section of Tientsin and taking control of this important centre which the allies needed as a base of operations to relieve Peking.

On 15 June a military council was convened on board the Russian flagship *Rossia*, one of the allied ships which were lying at anchor 10 miles offshore. Those present included Commander C.G.F.M. Craddock, officer commanding British naval forces in Seymour's absence, Vice-Admiral Bendemann, commander of the German Squadron in the Far East, and Rear-Admiral Courrejolles in command of the French Division in Chinese Waters. It met to consider the latest intelligence – that 2,000 rebels might cut the line to Tientsin, were poised to take over the Taku Forts from the Imperial troops, and had begun mining the Peiho River. On the previous day, reports had reached the coast that Baron von Ketteler, the German minister, had been killed in Peking. He was the second diplomat to die, the Japanese chancellor, Akira Sugiyama, having also died under suspicious circumstances. The information came not by telegraph, which had been cut, but by word of mouth and its reliability was therefore subject to question. Some substantiation came in the form of a press release circulated by the respected Laffan's News Agency through a telegraphic report. The London *Times* picked up the report and published, it adding further credence to the rumour. Surprisingly, the press release Laffan's issued on 16 June predated von Ketteler's death by four days, providing one of the many enigmas of the rebellion.

The situation came to a head when Chinese Imperial troops were seen occupying the railway and laying mines in the river. At another council meeting on 16 June, the admirals resolved to take immediate offensive action by capturing the Taku Forts. These were five forts on the Gulf of Pechihli located at the mouth of the Peiho River; two were situated on the north bank – No. 1 known as the North Fort, and No. 4 known as the Northwest (or inner) Fort. The remaining three were on the southern bank – Nos. 2, 3 and 5 known collectively as the South Forts. All were garrisoned by troops of the Imperial army. The forts were well known to the allies, having been stormed forty years earlier, although the defences had been improved considerably since then.

The Taku Forts photographed by Nathan J. Sargent, a clerk in the office of the American Trading Company who was a talented amateur photographer. His work frequently appeared in accounts published after the Peking siege. Sargent was in Tientsin during the siege of that place and was a member of the volunteers. (Jean S. and Frederic A. Sharf Collection)

Significantly the large guns of the forts pointed out to sea, making them useless against any attack coming from inland.

Following the meeting, the admirals gave the Chinese an option to surrender the forts peacefully by calling on the Governor of Chihli Province to hand them over but stating that if he declined, the forts would be taken by force. While the deadline was set for 2.00am on 17 June, the allies anticipating a rejection had begun to land troops near Tongku Railway Station further up the river. At 3.15pm on the afternoon of 16 June, 180 Russians were landed and 45 minutes later, 250 British and 130 German soldiers and marines followed. Three hundred Japanese troops were also landed to act as a reserve and were joined by some small contingents from Austria and Italy. Several gunboats had also moved into place. By early evening the situation had become critical as there was no sign that the Chinese intended to surrender the forts.

The entrance to the Peiho River was blocked by a sand bar which meant that only smaller ships could enter. Ten allied ships took up position inside the bar while the remainder of the fleet lay out in the

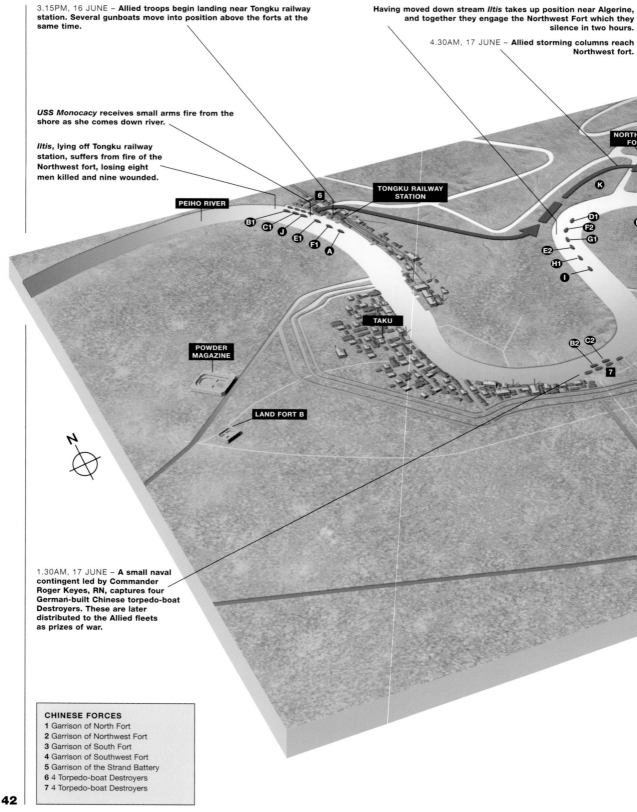

3.15PM, 16 JUNE – **Allied troops begin landing near Tongku railway station. Several gunboats move into position above the forts at the same time.**

Having moved down stream *Iltis* takes up position near Algerine, and together they engage the Northwest Fort which they silence in two hours.

4.30AM, 17 JUNE – **Allied storming columns reach Northwest fort.**

USS Monocacy receives small arms fire from the shore as she comes down river.

Iltis, lying off Tongku railway station, suffers from fire of the Northwest fort, losing eight men killed and nine wounded.

NORTHW
FORT

PEIHO RIVER

6

TONGKU RAILWAY
STATION

B1 C1 J E1 F1 A

K

D1
F2
E3
G1
E2
H1
I

TAKU

POWDER
MAGAZINE

B2 C2
7

LAND FORT B

N

1.30AM, 17 JUNE – **A small naval contingent led by Commander Roger Keyes, RN, captures four German-built Chinese torpedo-boat Destroyers. These are later distributed to the Allied fleets as prizes of war.**

CHINESE FORCES
1 Garrison of North Fort
2 Garrison of Northwest Fort
3 Garrison of South Fort
4 Garrison of Southwest Fort
5 Garrison of the Strand Battery
6 4 Torpedo-boat Destroyers
7 4 Torpedo-boat Destroyers

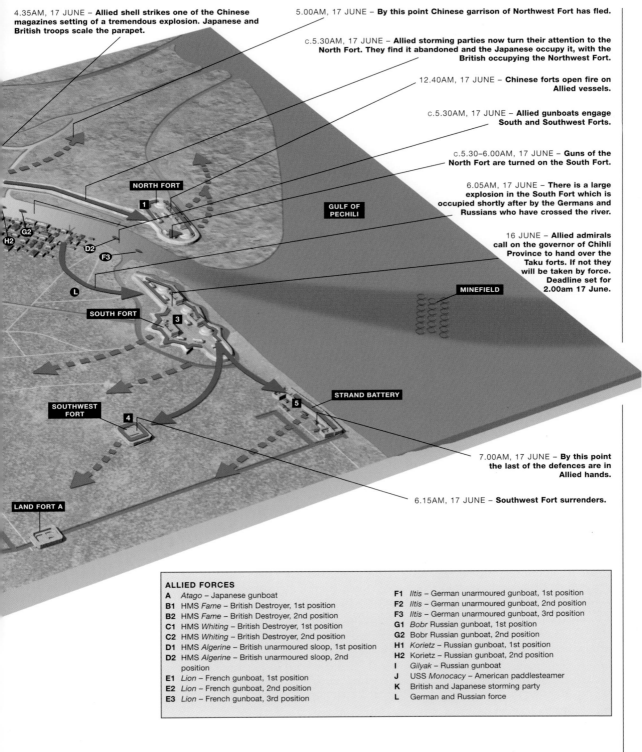

4.35AM, 17 JUNE – Allied shell strikes one of the Chinese magazines setting of a tremendous explosion. Japanese and British troops scale the parapet.

5.00AM, 17 JUNE – By this point Chinese garrison of Northwest Fort has fled.

c.5.30AM, 17 JUNE – Allied storming parties now turn their attention to the North Fort. They find it abandoned and the Japanese occupy it, with the British occupying the Northwest Fort.

12.40AM, 17 JUNE – Chinese forts open fire on Allied vessels.

c.5.30AM, 17 JUNE – Allied gunboats engage South and Southwest Forts.

c.5.30–6.00AM, 17 JUNE – Guns of the North Fort are turned on the South Fort.

6.05AM, 17 JUNE – There is a large explosion in the South Fort which is occupied shortly after by the Germans and Russians who have crossed the river.

16 JUNE – Allied admirals call on the governor of Chihli Province to hand over the Taku forts. If not they will be taken by force. Deadline set for 2.00am 17 June.

7.00AM, 17 JUNE – By this point the last of the defences are in Allied hands.

6.15AM, 17 JUNE – Southwest Fort surrenders.

NORTH FORT

GULF OF PECHILI

MINEFIELD

SOUTH FORT

SOUTHWEST FORT

STRAND BATTERY

LAND FORT A

ALLIED FORCES

A	*Atago* – Japanese gunboat	**F1**	*Iltis* – German unarmoured gunboat, 1st position
B1	HMS *Fame* – British Destroyer, 1st position	**F2**	*Iltis* – German unarmoured gunboat, 2nd position
B2	HMS *Fame* – British Destroyer, 2nd position	**F3**	*Iltis* – German unarmoured gunboat, 3rd position
C1	HMS *Whiting* – British Destroyer, 1st position	**G1**	*Bobr* Russian gunboat, 1st position
C2	HMS *Whiting* – British Destroyer, 2nd position	**G2**	Bobr Russian gunboat, 2nd position
D1	HMS *Algerine* – British unarmoured sloop, 1st position	**H1**	*Korietz* – Russian gunboat, 1st position
D2	HMS *Algerine* – British unarmoured sloop, 2nd position	**H2**	Korietz – Russian gunboat, 2nd position
		I	*Gilyak* – Russian gunboat
E1	*Lion* – French gunboat, 1st position	**J**	USS *Monocacy* – American paddlesteamer
E2	*Lion* – French gunboat, 2nd position	**K**	British and Japanese storming party
E3	*Lion* – French gunboat, 3rd position	**L**	German and Russian force

CAPTURE OF THE TAKU FORTS

16–17 June 1900, viewed from the south west, showing the combined attack by gunboats and storming parties and the capture of the forts themselves

Gulf. What the allies had demanded was viewed as an act of war by the Chinese, and observing the allied ships moving up the Peiho River, the forts opened fire at 12.40am on Sunday 17 June. They targeted the old iron Japanese gunboat *Atago*, the modern British destroyers HMS *Fame* and *Whiting* accompanying the unarmoured sloop HMS *Algerine*, the old French gunboat *Lion*, the USS *Monocacy*, an old American wooden paddle-steamer built in 1863, the German unarmoured vessel *Iltis*, and the Russian ships *Bobr* – an old steel gunboat armed with muzzle-loading weapons – the *Korietz*, which was similar, and the *Gilyak*, a modern gunboat. A number of civilian vessels were tied up along the wharves at Taku and an officer on board one ship, the SS *Hsin-Fung*, Chief Officer Gordon, described some of the ensuing action: 'One of the Russians got a shot in her bow and is now aground in shallow water. She was hit five times in all and another of the Russians was hit three times. The *Algerine*, a British vessel, sustained no serious damage and only took two shots through her stoke-hold ventilators … the USS *Monocacy* had been up river on patrol work, and as she came down men on shore near the wharves opened fire on her with rifles but they were soon silenced.' The *Iltis* lying off Tongku Railway Station suffered severely from the fire of the Northwest Fort and lost 8 men killed and nine wounded, but shortly afterwards moved down river and took up a position near the *Algerine* and together they engaged the fort, which they silenced in two hours.

Word was now sent to the allied landing parties to commence the assault on the forts. Advancing in echelon of columns they arrived at the Northwest Fort around 4.30am. Five minutes later there was a tremendous explosion as an allied shell struck one of the Chinese magazines which blew up. British and Japanese troops scaled the parapet and captured the fort and by 5.00am the Chinese garrison had fled. The gunboats now turned their attention on the North Fort and the landing parties found it to have been abandoned. Both the forts on the north bank were now occupied by allied troops, the North Fort by the Japanese and the Northwest Fort by the British. Other allied gunboats lying just below the dockyard at Taku engaged the South and Southwest Forts, while the guns of the North Fort were also trained across the river. At 6.05am there was a large explosion in the South Fort, which was occupied shortly after by the Germans and Russians who had crossed the river. The last of the defences was in allied hands by 7.00am. A total of 904 allied soldiers and sailors had taken part in the operation and casualties had been slight; the British lost one killed and nine wounded while the Russians had five officers and 28 men killed and another 60 wounded. While the allied vessels had sustained some damage, it was minor and the most momentous naval event was the capture of four German-built Chinese torpedo-boat destroyers lying at anchor, by a small naval contingent led by Commander Roger Keyes at 1.30am.

THE SIEGE OF TIENTSIN

BELOW **Another version of the capture of the one of the Taku forts. The marshes surrounding the forts, particularly on the landward side of the Northwest and North forts, presented an obstacle to the allies but were overcome with little difficulty, and several of the forts were abandoned without a fight. (Anne S.K. Brown Military Collection, Brown University Library)**

Tientsin was considered an important commercial city by foreign merchants. It was well situated on the Peiho River at the junction with the Grand Canal approximately 30 miles distant from Taku. In 1900 the Foreign Concession consisted of three distinct western communities: British, French and German. Another community of Japanese business people was developing into a fourth foreign enclave. The environment they created was very civilised with handsome buildings, roads, gas lights, parks, and churches, and was completely separate from the native Chinese. When the rebellion erupted the city was an obvious target.

Viewed as an important base of operations for any advance on Peking, it was vital that the city be secured. Seymour had gathered his force here before heading north and on 13 June, shortly after his departure, allied troops began to arrive including 1,700 Russian infantry, 150 mounted Cossacks and 4 field guns under Lieutenant Colonel Anisimoff. Aware of this build-up the Boxers cut the telegraph wire to Taku on the 15th and occupied the Native City. On the previous day a courier had arrived from Peking reporting that all mission houses in the Western Hills, and the Summer Legation had been burnt. Also on 14 June the Russians sent a force to Chun Liang Cheng to hold the station. There were estimated to be in the range of 10,000 Boxers and Imperial troops with 60 modern guns in and around the Native City of Tientsin.

Captain Edward H. Bayly of HMS *Aurora*, one of the garrison in Tientsin, noted in his journal on 16 June: 'The Boxers made an attack on Settlement early in morning and set fire to houses … they had cover from Native City from native houses until close to Concession. The Boxers also attacked the Railway Station, but were driven off by Russian guard'. A train was sent out towards

Tongku but came under heavy shell fire and was forced to return. On 17 June another train was sent out to repair lines and found itself cut off by a large body of Chinese. The troops on board opened fire with a 6-pdr gun and were able to return. An attack was made the same day by allied troops on the Chinese Military College just as the Chinese began to fire the first shells into the foreign settlements. The College was captured and set on fire and a battery of 3-in. guns taken.

Over the next six days the Concession was subjected to almost continuous bombardment and the Chinese made attacks on the railway station and other points, but were beaten off by allied troops from a total garrison of 2,400 troops. Within the foreign settlements themselves, the civilians had built barricades and earthworks, many of them constructed under the direction of Herbert Hoover, the future President of the United States. The cellars of the Municipal Hall, considered bomb-proof, were hastily adapted to accommodate women and children. There was a little relief when some of the besieging force moved north to block Seymour's retreat, relaxing the pressure on Tientsin although the bombardment resumed, as Captain Bayly noted on 21 June: 'A heavy bombardment. Having only the abominable 9-pdr muzzle-loading field gun and 6-pdr quick-firing available, can do

ABOVE **The Weihaiwei Regiment landing at Taku from Hong Kong in a photograph published in August 1900. They provided good service under British officers at Tientsin having reached the city on 24 June. They also took part in the attack on the Hsiku Arsenal to relieve Seymour's force. (Anne S.K. Brown Military Collection, Brown University Library)**

RIGHT **Mrs Lou Hoover standing by one of the guns in the defences of Tientsin during the siege. Her husband, Herbert, the future President of the United States, was a mining engineer who played an important part in the siege and was responsible for laying out many of the fortifications. He supervised the Chinese in erecting street barricades made from sacks of rice, sugar and peanuts taken from local warehouses, His wife volunteered as a nurse in the hospital established in the Tientsin Club. (Herbert Hoover Presidential Library, West Branch, Iowa)**

little to annoy or silence guns in Native City. The black smoke gives away the 9-pdr, and its range is poor. The 6-pdr quick-firing is useful in scattering parties of Chinese to the westward.'

An advance force of 500 allied troops from Taku attempted to break through to Tientsin but were checked about four miles from the foreign settlements and had to fall back. Meanwhile north of the city, Seymour's force was attempting to return. Preparations were made by the garrison to assist Seymour and as many troops as could be spared were sent out, leaving precariously few defenders. Fortunately, the situation was alleviated when 8,000 allied sailors, marines and soldiers finally broke through the Chinese lines from the south and entered Tientsin on 23 June, and on the following day, a group of Russians under General Stessel, and the First Chinese Regiment, known also as the Weihaiwei

ABOVE A photograph entitled 'Silencing the enemy's artillery', shows Lieutenant Drummond, Royal Navy, and the 12-pdr gun crew from HMS *Terrible* in action at Tientsin; they had been at the siege of Ladysmith earlier in the year. Captain Edward Bayly noted that the arrival of this gun was a most welcome addition as their only other gun, a 9-pdr, gave away their position because of the thick smoke from its black powder. (Anne S.K. Brown Military Collection, Brown University Library)

LEFT 'Illustration of the Charge of the 11th Infantry Regiment during the Destruction of the South Gate by Our Army when Attacking Tientsin Castle'. Coloured lithograph printed on 20 August 1900, and published three days later by Fukuda of Tokyo. Most Japanese prints of the period were based purely on imagination with no resemblance to actuality. (Anne S.K. Brown Military Collection, Brown University Library)

Regiment, arrived in the city. Seymour's column was found at the Hsiku Arsenal by Cossacks and escorted back to Tientsin, arriving on the 25th to find much of the city in ruins and the streets barricaded. Many of the buildings in the Concessions had been damaged or destroyed either by shellfire or by fire. The increased force now available enabled the allies to go on the offensive and they destroyed the Tientsin Arsenal

on 27 June and other places occupied by the Boxers, but on 28th the Chinese resumed their bombardment and from then on until 12 July Tientsin was once again under some form of siege. Both sides attempted to gain the upper hand, the Chinese staging an unsuccessful attack on the railway station on 4 July. The allies recaptured the Hsiku Arsenal which had been taken by the Chinese, on the 9th, and a three hour battle took place on the 11th which resulted in numerous allied casualties.

Finally, on 13 July the allies attacked the Chinese Native City. The attack was made from two directions. On the right were the Russians along with a few Germans and French who moved around to the east and north; the left attack consisted of Japanese, British, Americans and other allies, and the remaining French who moved out from the Settlements and worked their way around to the southwest and up to the South Gate of the city. The attack commenced around four in the

morning and as the allies moved in, they were met by a blistering fire. The walled city was captured the next day at a very high cost to the allies but they took a terrible revenge on the Chinese for the rumoured murder of all the foreigners in Peking, news of which had reached the allies just prior to the attack. The capture of Tientsin was a terrible blow to the Chinese and it was made worse by the death of General Nieh Shih-ch'eng, considered by many to have been the ablest of the Chinese commanders.

Russian and German positions for the attack on 13 July.

Germans

Russians

Russians

Chinese

East Arsenal

Chinese Camps

27 June. Allied forces attack the East Arsenal, one of the largest arsenals in northern China. Chinese forces are driven from the arsenal which is occupied by the Russians.

Chinese Garrison

Mud wall

Germans

British, Americans, Japanese & French

German Marines

Reserve

Chinese

Mud wall

Russian Concessions

Belgian Concessions

Military College

Peiho River

Tientsin University

International Bridge

American Concessions

British Concessions

French Concessions

Canal

Railway Station

Lutai Canal

Italian Concessions

Austrian Concessions

Blackfort

Mud wall

23 June. Route of Allied Relief Column.

Chinese Camps

Japanese Concessions

Japanese

Americans

Western Arsenal

French

Reserve

Americans

British

Japanese

Racecourse

Hsiku Arsenal

Grand Canal

Tientsin

Chinese

Mud wall

Chinese

Hsiho River

Canal

Mud wall

13 July. Allied forces attack the Chinese city of Tientsin. They meet fierce resistance heavy fire. Many units are pinned down and suffer heavy casualties. After nightfall many units withdraw, but the Japanese courageously hold onto their forward position and around 3.00am Japanese sappers blew open the south gate. Allied forces captured the city in a swift attack on 14 July.

| 0 | 2 miles |
| 0 | 4 km |

N

51

THE SIEGE OF PEKING

The Semi-Siege

The news that everyone in the foreign legations at Peking had been killed began to reach the foreign capitals around the middle of July 1900. The London *Graphic* echoed everyone's feelings when it reported on 21 July: 'For it is no longer to be doubted that on or about July 9, the Chinese capital was the scene of an outrage on humanity and the comity of nations which has been called the greatest crime of the century, but which might almost be described as the foulest crime of all the centuries.' It went on to compare the so-called massacre with the similar events at Lucknow and Cawnpore during the Indian Mutiny. Naturally there was horror and outrage, and calls for the Chinese to be dealt with swiftly. Plans were made in London for a memorial service to be held in St. Paul's Cathedral on Monday 23 July but doubts began to arise as to the validity of the reports coming out of China and the Dean of the cathedral prudently decided to cancel the event.

In Tientsin the victorious allies had also heard about the apparent massacre in Peking. If it was true, and they had no reason to doubt it, there was little urgency to move rapidly on the capital. In addition the commanders were hesitant to make any further rash decisions following the experience of Seymour's expedition. Instead, they decided to build up their forces before advancing on Peking, although plans for their departure were delayed to allow all the foreign contingents presently en route to China to arrive.

In reality, the foreign ministers and their families were still alive and holding out in Peking. Following MacDonald's plea for help on 9 June, the foreign community in the capital had waited anxiously for the arrival

The Peitang Cathedral held by a small contingent of French and Italian sailors who protected over 3,000 Catholics including priests, nuns and native converts. This place withstood violent attacks from the Chinese but held out until relieved by Japanese troops on 15 August 1900. Parts of the adjacent buildings were badly damaged by several explosions triggered by the Chinese. (Anne S.K. Brown Military Collection, Brown University Library)

of a relief column even dispatching wagons to the railway station to provide transportation for the anticipated allied troops. As the days passed and the relief failed to materialise, a sense of gloom descended on the foreign compound. The murder of the Japanese Chancellor, Sugiyama, on the 11th outside the Yung Ting Men gate by Imperial soldiers only served to make matters worse. When the ministers protested, the answer was that the murder was the work of bandits. Two days later a group of Chinese agitators were attacked by the German minister, Baron von Ketteler. It was enough to convince the foreigners that Boxers had now infiltrated the streets close by and it was determined to post guards and send others over to the large Roman Catholic cathedral of Peitang. The first fortifications went up. To compound matters smallpox had broken out and a number of foreigners had come down with it. Two defensive positions were now established in Peking – at the Legation Quarter, and at the Peitang Cathedral. The population of both were swollen with Chinese converts and missionaries who had fled into Peking from the countryside where murder and other outrages had been committed.

On 14 June Boxers burned missionary chapels and shops selling foreign goods but were charged by some of the American marines as well as being shot down by other guards on Legation Street. The following day, thousands of Chinese surged against the southern walls of the city chanting 'Sha, sha, sha' ('Kill, kill, kill'). Private Oscar Upham of the United States Marine Corps, wrote in his diary: 'Ten American marines and twenty Russians from the Legations marched down to the Nam Tong (or South Church) and found some Boxers killing and torturing some Chinese Christians. Our boys killed about 50 and rescued 300 Christians, many of them wounded … we received word that [Admiral Seymour] at the head of 2,000 foreign sailors and marines were on their way from Tientsin to relieve us.' Over 4,000 businesses went up in flames on 16 June and later in the day the Ch'ien Men gate was consumed by fire. The foreign quarter would have suffered the same fate had it not been for the stone wall which separated it from the Chinese City.

Intent on frightening the foreigners into submission, the Chinese sent word on 18 June that they were going to gather 80,000 men to attack the Legations on the 27th. This was no doubt a direct response to the bombardment and capture of the Taku Forts the previous day. The storming of the forts certainly led the Tsungli Yamen to demand at 4.00pm on 19 June that all foreigners quit the city as their safety could not be guaranteed. The Tsungli Yamen informed the ministers that the allied admirals had demanded the surrender of the Taku Forts though they did not admit that the forts had already been captured, and added that 'this is an act of war. Our country is therefore at war with yours. You must accordingly quit our capital within twenty-four hours accompanied by all your nationals'. The ministers met to discuss this critical impasse and unsure of the situation on the coast or with the progress of the relief column, decided to play for time by requesting a meeting at the Tsungli Yamen the next day. Gathering at the French Legation on 20 June, they awaited word from the foreign ministry. Lancelot Giles, a student interpreter at the British Legation, described what happened next: 'At 9am came some very sad news. The ministers were to have gone

The British Legation Compound photographed by Revd C.A. Killie during the siege of the Legation Quarter. This view is taken from across the canal towards the barricaded entrance of the British Legation. One of the hastily built barricades made of wagons and furniture can be seen stretching across the dry bed of the canal. (Jean S. and Frederic A. Sharf Collection)

to a meeting at the Tsungli Yamen. They decided not to go; but the German Minister, Baron von Ketteler, and his interpreter Cordes went in chairs. They had not gone far before they were fired on from all sides by Chinese soldiers. The bearers dropped the chairs and fled.' Von Ketteler was killed and his interpreter badly wounded in the incident. This crime incensed the Germans and the Kaiser, who demanded a leading role in the prosecution of the war. Later the same day, Professor Huberty James of the Imperial University was shot dead crossing the bridge over the canal near the British Legation.

Von Ketteler's murder convinced the ministers that staying in the capital was safer than heading south across open country with no protection. On the day of his death a note arrived from the foreign ministry asking the ministers to reconsider the ultimatum, but the decision had been made and the foreigners prepared for the worst. At 4.00pm the Chinese opened fire on the Legation Quarter and for the next 55 days until 14 August, the foreign community in Peking would be in a state of almost continuous siege.

THE SIEGE OF PEKING – FIRST STAGE

The foreign nationals quickly drew up plans for their defence and protection. William Ker, Assistant Chinese Secretary at the British Legation, in a letter written on 25 June described some of these plans: 'We have a General Committee to supervise all internal arrangements, subdivided into Fortifications, Sanitation, Commissariat, Registration, and so on, but it has not yet got into very smooth working order. Chinese labour is supplied by refugees from the Nantang etc. who are deposited in the Fu opposite but they are poorly fed and hardly worked.' He went

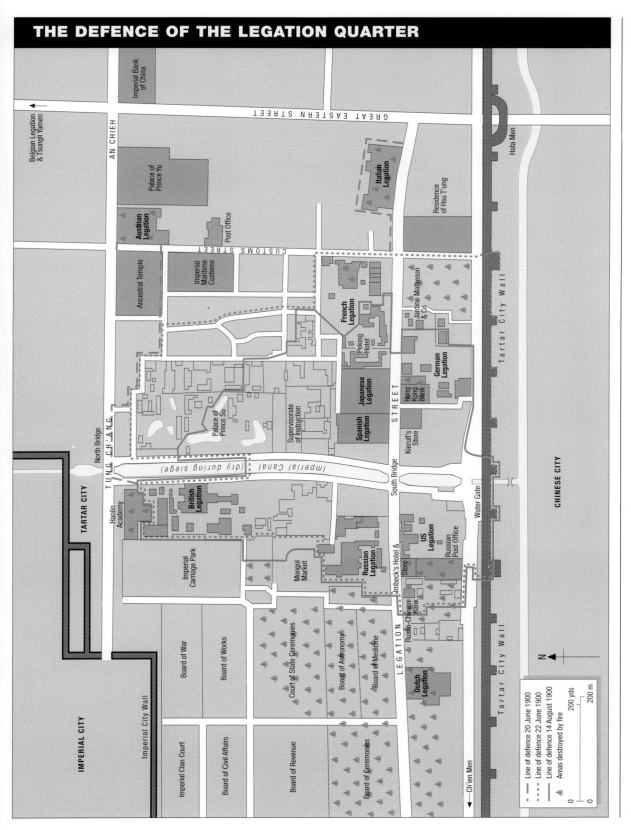

Belgian Legation & Tsungli Yamen

Imperial Bank of China

GREAT EASTERN STREET

Hata Men

AN CHIEH

Palace of Prince Yu

Italian Legation

Residence of Hsu Tung

Austrian Legation

Post Office

Ancestral Temple

Imperial Maritime Customs

CUSTOMS STREET

Jardine Matheson & Co

French Legation

Peking Hotel

German Legation

Hong Kong Bank

Japanese Legation

S T R E E T

Supervisorate of Instruction

Spanish Legation

Palace of Prince Su

Kieruff's Store

North Bridge

TUNG CH'ANG

Imperial Canal (dry during siege)

South Bridge

Water Gate

CHINESE CITY

TARTAR CITY

Hanlin Academy

British Legation

Tartar City Wall

IMPERIAL CITY

Imperial City Wall

Imperial Carriage Park

Mongol Market

Russian Legation

Imbeck's Hotel & Store

US Legation

Russian Post Office

Board of War

Board of Works

Court of State Ceremonies

Board of Astronomy

Board of Medicine

L E G A T I O N

Russo-Chinese Bank

Dutch Legation

Tartar City Wall

Imperial Clan Court

Board of Civil Affairs

Board of Revenue

Board of Ceremonies

Ch'ien Men

N

Line of defence 20 June 1900
Line of defence 22 June 1900
Line of defence 14 August 1900
Areas destroyed by fire

0   200 yds
0   200 m

on: 'Bullets whizz over our heads all day and riddle the tops of the houses; today the Fortifications Committee has begun constructing bomb-proof shelters in case they start shelling us from the Ch'ien Men.' One committee was in charge of food supply and its efforts were greatly aided by the discovery in a shop on the corner of Legation Street of 8,000 bushels of new wheat recently brought in from Hunan. This unground wheat was carried on carts to the British Legation and it sustained the foreign community until the siege was lifted in mid-August 1900.

There were many committees but a glance at one will suffice to give an impression of the organisational skills brought to bear in this critical situation. The task of fortifying the Legation Quarter fell to Fortification Staff with the Chief of Staff being the very able Revd Frank D. Gamewell, assisted by Messrs. Chapin, Ewing, Killie, Norris, Smith, Stonehouse and others. Gamewell, an American missionary who had two years of engineering instruction and field work also understood the various forms of Chinese construction practices and the management of Chinese labour, skills that would put him in good stead during the defence operations. His efforts at successfully fortifying the Legation

Quarter, and in particular his fortifying of the British Legation compound, might have been the difference between life and death to the besieged. One colleague wrote: 'Early and late, by day and by night in the heat of the sun and in tropical rains, he gave undivided attention to the single problem of how to render the Legation as nearly impregnable as the serious natural disabilities of the situation rendered possible.'

One consideration was the difficulty of defending the large perimeter surrounding most of the Legations and it was decided to move all civilians other than the defenders of the Peitang Cathedral and the marines guarding the various other Legations into the British Legation, which was the largest and commanded a reasonable field of fire. It was also not overlooked by the Tartar Wall and therefore not immediately exposed to attack. The 3-acre compound, which normally housed around 60 persons, was turned into a central redoubt with loopholes, sandbagged emplacements on the walls and a barricade at the gateway, with space for 900 combatants and non-combatants alike along with sheep, horses and other assorted animals. To improve the field of fire, a defensive area was created by burning Chinese homes around the Legation. Luella Miner, an American professor, described watching people streaming in from the other Legations and all the foreign establishments on Legation Street, 'until the compound was a veritable Babel, seventeen nationalities being represented. Greek and Roman Catholic priests, French and Chinese nuns, soldiers in their

Posed photograph of the Fuel Supply Committee in the British Legation compound taken by Revd C. A. Killie after the siege. Killie took numerous posed photographs of various groups of siege participants, some taken during the siege, and others after it had ended. Following his return to America many of his photographs were used to illustrate various accounts of the siege. (Jean S. and Frederic A. Sharf Collection)

Posed group of American missionaries who had endured the siege, photographed by Revd C.A. Killie. These men and women were the backbone of the various committees throughout the siege and helped on the defences, in the hospital and in other critical tasks. Following their return home, several of them penned their experiences for articles and books. (Jean S. and Frederic A. Sharf Collection)

uniforms, made a unique scene.' Chinese converts estimated to be in the region of 2,700 persons were to be housed in the grounds of Prince Su's Palace (the Su Wang Fu) situated just across the Imperial Canal from the British Legation. The Belgian, Austrian, Dutch and Italian Legations, which lay outside the line of defence, were put to the torch.

The outer defensive perimeter ran south along the rear walls of the British and Russian Legation buildings up to and onto part of the city wall. Here it ran eastwards along the wall for 2,000 feet or so, before turning north towards the French Legation and other buildings and then following the road plan around the Su Palace to meet the canal just north of the British Legation by the Hanlin Academy. During the next few weeks and months, this perimeter would oscillate as buildings were given up or other points strengthened. And on two occasions, the stretch of wall defended by the allies was overrun only to be recaptured. Walls were loopholed, ditches dug with pointed wooden stakes set within and lined with barbed wire fences, observation platforms erected, and walls dug up for bricks to close gates and windows.

Inside the British compound itself everyone performed some duty whether it was working in the makeshift hospital, food procurement, sowing sandbags or guarding gateways. An American tourist, Anna Woodward, described the sandbag-making detail: 'We worked every Sunday but one or two during the long, weary weeks we were besieged. In many of the Chinese houses adjoining the British Legation were rolls and rolls of beautiful, costly silks and embroideries, and a glorious sight it was to see the silks brought in, and a glorious work it was to cut them up into bags for sand and protection. No one ever saw such barricades or ever will again.'

The 22 buildings of the compound were taken over by the international community and the military procured several for barracks. For instance, the bowling alley became home to the Royal Marine contingent, some of whom also shared the theatre with US Marines; the American Legation was now in the home of Dr. Poole, the Legation's physician, the Student Interpreter's quarters was occupied by the German, Japanese and Eurasians, while the gatehouse accommodated some Swedish and Portuguese citizens. To defend the outer perimeter and the Legation was a mixed force of soldiers, sailors and marines, backed up by volunteers, a total of just over 400 marine guards from eight countries and 75 armed volunteers in all. There were 82 men and

The elegant house of Henry Cockburn, Chinese Secretary of the British Legation responsible for training student interpreters, barricaded during the siege. Photograph by C.A. Killie. Private Haywood of the Rifle Brigade noted on 23 August 1900 that 'every building left standing was sandbagged up to the roof'. During the siege, Cockburn made his library available to the community. (Jean S. and Frederic A. Sharf Collection)

officers from Britain, 81 from Russia, 35 from Austria-Hungary, 48 Frenchmen, 51 Germans, 53 Americans, 29 Italians and 25 Japanese. Besides the volunteers, many of whom had some military experience, another group of 50 civilians calling themselves 'Thornhill's Rough's' served on the barricades. It fell to the British minister, Sir Claude MacDonald, to assume overall command of this ragtag force.

The task of defending the Peitang or North Cathedral situated inside the Imperial City near the west gate or the Hsi An Men was given to a small force of just over 40 French and Italian marines along with 13 French Fathers, 20 Sisters and 3,200 Chinese Christians, commanded by the French Monsignor Alphonse-Pierre Favier, the Vicar-Apostolic of Peking. Following the massacres at Paotingfu in May, he had stockpiled arms, stores and ammunition in anticipation of just such an event happening in the capital. He had said as much to the French minister, M. Pichon, and had ended with a plea for 'forty or fifty sailors, to protect our lives and our property'. Besides the cathedral itself, the compound included other miscellaneous buildings all of which had to be defended.

For the next ten days, the two compounds faced attacks from Boxer fanatics while the Chinese government and its army stayed on the sidelines. The cathedral was attacked on 15 June when 48 Chinese were killed. On 22 June, Boxers gathered near the barricade on Legation Street and began to loot the Dutch Legation but were soon cleared by gunfire. The next day, they looted and burned more shops in the Mongol Market and set fire to the Hanlin College just north of the British Legation, and the besieged began to be shot at by Chinese on the Tartar City wall; the Boxers also positioned a small 3-in. gun near the Legation Bank and started firing. Japanese and German marines killed many Boxers on 23 June and American marines charged along part of the Tartar Wall clearing the enemy almost as far as the burnt-out Ch'ien Men gate. An incident typical of the siege was the action of Captain L.S.T. Halliday of the Royal Marine Light Infantry who won a Victoria

The six 'Fighting Parsons' at Fort Cockburn, a wooden platform behind Cockburn's house on which the British Nordenfeldt gun was mounted; this was manned by Sergeant J. Murphy, Royal Marines (seated on the platform). Killie, the photographer, is the tall man standing at the rear of the group. This photograph was taken during the July truce. Reverend Stonehouse, the gentleman dressed entirely in white, was killed sometime after this photograph was taken. (Jean S. and Frederic A. Sharf Collection)

Cross for his endeavours. Sir Claude MacDonald noted this event: 'On the 24th, the enemy consisting of Boxers and Imperial troops made a fierce attack on the west wall of the British Legation, setting fire to the west gate of the south stable quarters, and taking cover in the building which adjoined the wall. The fire, which spread to part of the stables, and through which and the smoke a galling fire was kept up by the Imperial troops, was with difficulty extinguished, and as the presence of the enemy in the adjoining buildings was a grave danger to the Legation, Captain Strouts, with my sanction, and Captain Halliday, in command of 20 marines, led the way into the buildings and almost immediately engaged a party of the enemy.' Halliday was shot but not before he killed three Chinese and telling his men to carry on, he walked unaided to the hospital.

For the next few days the 3-in. gun and the snipers on the wall continued to rain havoc on the defenders, and from their own newly constructed barricades, the Chinese began to pour a steady stream of bullets into the allied line many of which were finding their mark as casualties began to mount. On 25 June the Chinese planted a sign stating: 'An Imperial command to protect ministers and to stop firing'. All firing ceased and the Chinese were seen building earthworks, but at midnight firing resumed with an increased intensity.

Day after day this exchange of fire continued with the occasional attacks and counter-attacks as Mrs E.K. Lowry noted in her diary entries: [29 June] 'Captain Wray (British) makes a sortie to the west, to capture the big gun that has been firing on us from there but is unsuccessful'; and 'To-day [1 July] the Germans are forced to give up their position on the wall. Only three were left to hold the position and it was too hard for them. This left the Americans so much exposed that they also retired, but later the position was retaken, Captain Wray being wounded in the attack.'

The wall of the Tartar City presented continual problems for the besieged as it directly overlooked the Legation Quarter and the Chinese

The improvised cannon known as 'Betsy', the 'International' or 'Boxer Bill' (other names for it included the 'Dowager Empress' and 'Old Crock') constructed during the siege from an antique cannon. The photograph was taken during the July truce by the Revd C.A. Killie; later the photograph appeared on the cover of *Leslie's Weekly* of 15 December 1900. This gun is now in the United States Marine Corps museum. (Jean S. and Frederic A. Sharf Collection)

were constantly sniping from it. Frequent sorties were made by the defenders to clear the Chinese but they always returned. On 24 June American marines had started to construct a barricade but on the following day had been forced to retreat. A position on the wall was maintained but precariously. On 1 July German defenders were driven from the wall and the Chinese continued to build barricades up on the battlements. On the following day, Private Upham noted that the Chinese had built a barricade within 60 feet of the defenders' position and shortly after, a tower was constructed and the Chinese began to throw large stones into the allied barricade. It was decided therefore to take offensive action. Upham described what happened next: 'At 2.30am Captain Myers and eight men went over the barricade and lay down; the Chinese opened up such a hot fire that the rest of the men were delayed in getting over, one Russian being wounded in the leg. The firing soon ceased and then the charge was made – our men yelling like Indians, Privates Turner and Thomas being in the lead, and as they gained the rear of the Chinese barricade they received a volley. Our men soon had the Chinks on the run and shot down about 60 of them. Captain Myers received a spear wound on the leg, poor Turner was found shot through the head and Thomas was hit in the stomach. Our men were quite busy throwing dead bodies over the wall into the Southern City.' Thereafter the defenders managed to maintain a hold on the stretch of wall between the Chien Men and Hata Men and were finally to capture the Chinese positions on 14 August enabling them to open the Chien Men gate to allow access to troops of the relief force.

On 7 July Mrs. Lowry noted the discovery of an 1860 vintage British 3-in. calibre smooth-bore gun in an old junk shop (although other

OVERLEAF: CAPTAIN MYERS' CHARGE ON THE TARTAR WALL, 3 JULY 1900.
'At 2.30am Captain Myers and eight men went over the barricade and lay down; the Chinese opened up such a hot fire that the rest of the men were delayed in getting over, one Russian being wounded in the leg. The firing soon ceased and then the charge was made – our men yelling like Indians, Privates Turner and Thomas being in the lead.' Private Oscar Upham, US Marine Corps. (Alan & Michael Perry)

A pavilion occupied by Hotel De
Pékin within the British Legation
compound during the siege,
photographed by C.A. Killie.
Because the Hotel formed part of
a dangerous sector of the outer
defences, the Swiss proprietors,
the Chamots, 'moved' the hotel
to a pavilion in the British
Legation, although Mrs Chamot
never left the original building
and her husband performed
valiant work in victualling the
besieged and later the relieving
forces. (Jean S. and Frederic A.
Sharf Collection)

diarists reported that it was found by Chinese converts while digging a trench). It was mounted on an Italian 1-pdr mount and for ammunition the Russians supplied some shrapnel and common shell which had been brought up from Tientsin by mistake instead of rifle ammunition. These 9-lb shells had been tossed down a well when the mistake was discovered but were fished out, dried and offered as ammunition for the newly nicknamed 'International', or 'Betsy' as she was fondly known. The shells were disassembled and used as two separate charges loaded through the muzzle by the two American marines who volunteered to fire it. The gun was taken over to the Su Wang Fu Palace, otherwise known as the Fu. 'We fired about a dozen shots with the old international', noted Private Upham, 'and did a lot of damage to Chinese barricades.' Thereafter the gun performed yeoman work for the defenders in bombarding the Imperial City walls and on one occasion destroyed a Chinese cannon. Later she was used to blow down a barricade in the Hanlin College immediately to the north of the British Legation. A description of the gun in *Leslie's Weekly* described one incident: 'One of her first bits of work was being hauled up the ramparts to the top of the city walls and fired into the Chinese barricade down by the great Meridian gate. As the shot struck and the bricks went flying, the Chinese were so surprised that they climbed up and looked over the barriers to see what had struck them, for up to that time they had believed that the besieged had nothing but rifles.'

The fighting continued unabated and it was now readily apparent to everyone that the enemy was now the Imperial army, the Boxers having faded into the background. A heavy bombardment continuously rained down on the Legation Quarter, where living conditions began to grow steadily worse, and to avoid injury 'bomb-proofs' were constructed. Dr. W.A.P. Martin, President of the Chinese Imperial University who served as a guard on one of the gates, described these dug-outs: 'They were barely large enough for the women and children: the men were expected to stand and fight the enemy. They were covered over with heavy beams, and these again with a stratum of earth and sand-bags. No cavern in a hillside could look more gloomy or forbidding.' The drought that had plagued the region for many months finally broke on 30 June and the torrential rain flooded out the 'bomb-proofs' and other trenches. Following the rain came the heat. which reached 110°F in the shade.

During the first week of July, attacks continued and there was no rest for the besieged. One missionary, J.H. Ross, described such an incident that occurred around 13 July: 'Just as I was writing last evening a furious attack began which lasted two hours or more – the most furious and long continued we have ever had. I was so glad it was not in the night. From one direction it was aimed especially at the French legation. The Chinese had mined under the house of the secretary of the legation and blew it up killing a number of their own people and burying two of the French in the ruins, and injuring several others. A great fire was started which burned several buildings, and the French were obliged to give up about half of their premises and fall back to another barricade. At the same time we were attacked from another direction, and the rifle-firing and cannonading were fearful, bullets, balls, and shells falling in all directions. In the midst of the general confusion a large company of Chinese – some 200 – were discovered creeping along close to the wall toward the American legation. They were fired upon by our troops, and 30 or 40 were killed. If we could all realize the situation it would be a fearful thing to feel one's self in the focus of all this murderous hate and devilry.'

On 14 July the Chinese attached a sheet of paper to a bridge announcing in large letters readable by telescope that 'we have received orders to protect the Foreign Ministers'. Incredibly they had called a truce just at the moment when the Chinese forces had the Legation Quarter in their grasp and could have taken it at any time. The garrison was losing men, particularly officers, every day and its ammunition

The entrance to a bomb-proof cellar in the British Legation compound is shown in the foreground of this photograph taken by Revd C.A. Killie. In the background can be seen the entrance to the Legation Chancery, which was used during the siege as a hospital. In the entrance sits Matron Lambert seated with two nursing assistants. (Jean S. and Frederic A. Sharf Collection)

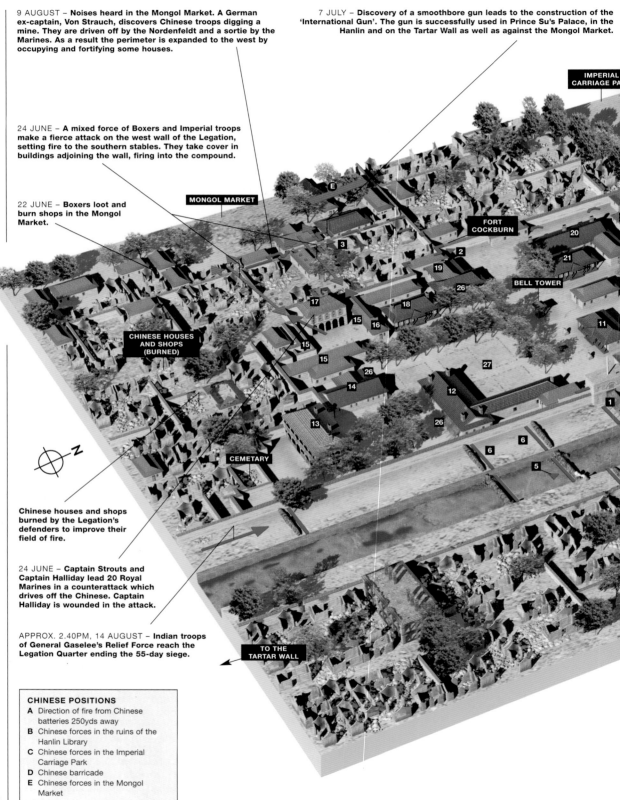

9 AUGUST – Noises heard in the Mongol Market. A German ex-captain, Von Strauch, discovers Chinese troops digging a mine. They are driven off by the Nordenfeldt and a sortie by the Marines. As a result the perimeter is expanded to the west by occupying and fortifying some houses.

7 JULY – Discovery of a smoothbore gun leads to the construction of the 'International Gun'. The gun is successfully used in Prince Su's Palace, in the Hanlin and on the Tartar Wall as well as against the Mongol Market.

24 JUNE – A mixed force of Boxers and Imperial troops make a fierce attack on the west wall of the Legation, setting fire to the southern stables. They take cover in buildings adjoining the wall, firing into the compound.

22 JUNE – Boxers loot and burn shops in the Mongol Market.

IMPERIAL CARRIAGE PAR

MONGOL MARKET

FORT COCKBURN

BELL TOWER

CHINESE HOUSES AND SHOPS (BURNED)

CEMETARY

Chinese houses and shops burned by the Legation's defenders to improve their field of fire.

24 JUNE – Captain Strouts and Captain Halliday lead 20 Royal Marines in a counterattack which drives off the Chinese. Captain Halliday is wounded in the attack.

APPROX. 2.40PM, 14 AUGUST – Indian troops of General Gaselee's Relief Force reach the Legation Quarter ending the 55-day siege.

TO THE TARTAR WALL

CHINESE POSITIONS
- **A** Direction of fire from Chinese batteries 250yds away
- **B** Chinese forces in the ruins of the Hanlin Library
- **C** Chinese forces in the Imperial Carriage Park
- **D** Chinese barricade
- **E** Chinese forces in the Mongol Market

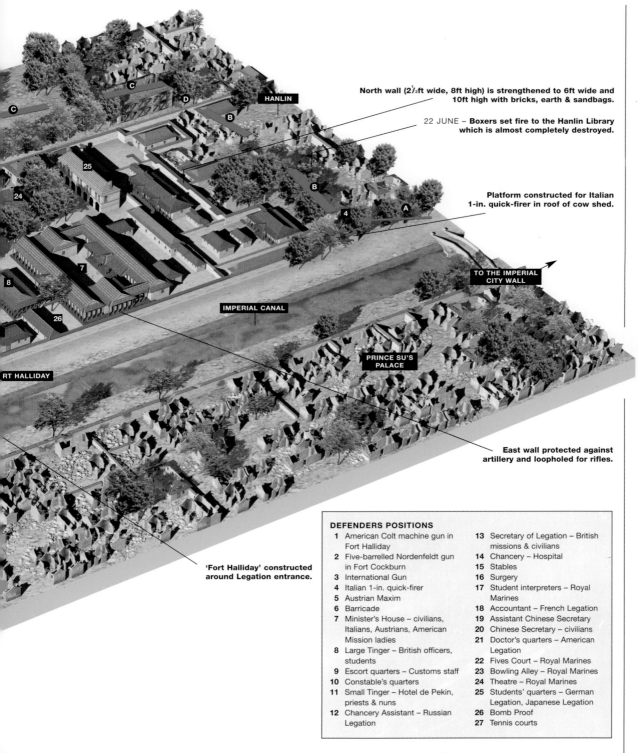

North wall (2½ft wide, 8ft high) is strengthened to 6ft wide and 10ft high with bricks, earth & sandbags.

22 JUNE – Boxers set fire to the Hanlin Library which is almost completely destroyed.

Platform constructed for Italian 1-in. quick-firer in roof of cow shed.

HANLIN

TO THE IMPERIAL CITY WALL

IMPERIAL CANAL

PRINCE SU'S PALACE

RT HALLIDAY

East wall protected against artillery and loopholed for rifles.

'Fort Halliday' constructed around Legation entrance.

DEFENDERS POSITIONS

1 American Colt machine gun in Fort Halliday
2 Five-barrelled Nordenfeldt gun in Fort Cockburn
3 International Gun
4 Italian 1-in. quick-firer
5 Austrian Maxim
6 Barricade
7 Minister's House – civilians, Italians, Austrians, American Mission ladies
8 Large Tinger – British officers, students
9 Escort quarters – Customs staff
10 Constable's quarters
11 Small Tinger – Hotel de Pekin, priests & nuns
12 Chancery Assistant – Russian Legation
13 Secretary of Legation – British missions & civilians
14 Chancery – Hospital
15 Stables
16 Surgery
17 Student interpreters – Royal Marines
18 Accountant – French Legation
19 Assistant Chinese Secretary
20 Chinese Secretary – civilians
21 Doctor's quarters – American Legation
22 Fives Court – Royal Marines
23 Bowling Alley – Royal Marines
24 Theatre – Royal Marines
25 Students' quarters – German Legation, Japanese Legation
26 Bomb Proof
27 Tennis courts

DEFENCE OF THE BRITISH LEGATION COMPOUND

20 June – 14 August 1900, viewed from the south west, showing the defences of the Legation compound and the approximate positions of the Chinese besiegers

A view of the interior of the British Legation compound photographed by Killie during the siege. It shows a bulletin board on the left and a chapel occupied by American missionaries on the right. Daily bulletins were posted in the Legation throughout the duration of the siege providing what information had been received on the progress of the relief forces . (Jean S. and Frederic A. Sharf Collection)

supply was dwindling. The Chinese were probably unaware of this critical situation and sensing a stalemate as well as the successes of the allied forces on the coast, decided to make friendly overtures. A letter that was brought in stated that Prince Ch'ing and his colleagues were pleased to hear that the ministers and their families were well, and suggested that the foreign ministers should go to the Tsungli Yamen. On the same day, a small supply of melons, vegetables and other food was sent into the allied quarter and news was exchanged, some of it relating to the relief force, which apparently was on its way although in actuality there was no relief force at that moment. Prior to this, some news had been received. A Chinese prisoner captured by the French on 12 July revealed that the foreign settlements at Tientsin had been burned on 16 June and the Taku forts captured on the 17th.

While life became a little more tolerable in the allied perimeter, the proposed meeting with the Chinese never materialised as MacDonald had politely declined to meet with them fearing for the safety of his colleagues. There was desultory fighting over the next few days, and some cannonading at night, and several lives were lost by stray shot. Captain Strouts of the Royal Marines who commanded the British contingent and served as MacDonald's chief of staff, was caught in a hail of bullets on the morning of 16 July, and was buried along with a young customs worker who had been mortally wounded the day before. On the whole however the Chinese attacks were less vigorous. A second letter from Prince Ch'ing arrived on the 15th assuring the ministers that the Chinese government would 'continue to exert all its efforts to keep order and give protection', and requesting that if the allied troops stopped firing, the Chinese would do the same. A telegram in cipher also came in addressed to the US minister, Edwin Conger, saying only 'Communicate to bearer'. What this meant nobody knew but it may have signified a split in the Chinese government with Prince Ch'ing and Jung Lu and his troops wishing to preserve the foreign community, while Prince Tuan and Lung Fu Hriang and their troops determined to destroy them. The build-up of foreign troops on the coast certainly influenced their actions, Whatever the reason, on 17 July the guns fell silent and a strange truce prevailed.

The July Truce

With the truce soldiers from both sides began to fraternise, inspect each other's barricades and exchange cigarettes and fruit. MacDonald took stock of his defences on 21 July: 'French and German Legations, Russian and British Legations, half the park of the British Legation and the centre of the American Legation. Everything outside these lines in ruins. All the dwellings have been burnt down and large spaces have been levelled.' The defenders began to relax their vigilance and instead indulged in sports and other more peaceful pursuits. Spirits were lifted when a letter which had reached the Japanese on 18 July was posted on the Bell Tower in the British compound which served as the posting station for all news; it read 'The Japanese Minister has received news to the following effect. A mixed division consisting of 2,400 Japanese, 4,000 Russians, 2,000 British, 1,500 Americans, 1,500 French, and 300 Germans, leave Tientsin on or about 20th instant for the relief of Peking. The foreign settlement of Tientsin has not been taken by the enemy.' While it was welcome news it meant that relief was still days away.

An imaginary scene entitled 'Heroic Defence of the British Legation at Pekin' painted by the German artist Fritz Neumann. Such images, while full of action, provided a false impression of the actual conditions during the siege. While there were a few close encounters, most of the siege involved bombardments and sniping by the Chinese. The picture does try to convey the multi-national make-up of the garrison. (Anne S.K. Brown Military Collection, Brown University Library)

THE DEFENCE OF THE BRITISH LEGATION
The British Legation was the lynchpin of the defence of the Legation district. All the non-combatants were gathered here including women, children and Chinese Christians. Defended by a mixture of Royal Marines, some 'bluejackets' and assorted civilian volunteers, it was heavily attacked on numerous occasions with much of the fighting taking place in the area of the Hanlin Academy, the Mongol Market and Prince Su's Palace. (Alan & Michael Perry)

A lull fell over the battlefield and as one lady wrote on the 19th, 'we have had twenty-four hours of absolute quiet, no sound of shot or shell, and it seems strange to lie down to sleep without our customary serenade and to be able to walk about the compound without wondering whether a shell will burst over our heads'. Throughout this period, MacDonald was in constant communication with the Tsungli Yamen, and more communications were exchanged between the factions, the latest from the Chinese blaming the whole affair on the Boxers and the ministers requesting that they be allowed to communicate with their governments, but the Chinese responded that the telegraph lines to Tientsin had been cut. They did suggest that the foreign ministers travel to Tientsin under guard.

The truce allowed the besieged to replenish their food supplies and there was an active trade in eggs between the belligerents. More fruit was sent in on 25 July by order of the Empress Dowager. Nonetheless, conditions were far from ideal and the heat and mosquitoes made life intolerable. During this period the Chinese erected more fortifications including a six-foot barricade over a bridge at the foot of the Imperial City wall just north of the British Legation and continued mining operations, occasionally firing off some ammunition for fear that the foreigners were planning something. This was always attributed by the Tsungli Yamen in its correspondence with MacDonald to misunderstandings. US Marine Private Upham noted on 26 July, 'the Chinese are very suspicious and kept burning rockets all night which illuminated the whole place; there was occasional firing all night', but on the 29th things changed for the worse as Upham noted: 'The war is on again in earnest. The Chinese started it by picking off some of our coolies; we retaliated by picking a few of them off their roost. This brought on a general engagement. We feel better, having something to do, than we did during the truce.'

THE SIEGE OF PEKING – SECOND STAGE

August began as July finished with both sides exchanging occasional fire but there was still no sign of the anticipated relief force. 'Another month begun! Where can the relief force be?' wrote Lancelot Giles on 1 August. A census of the British Legation on this day read: Soldiers, British and others – 73; General Hospital, wounded – 40; Legation residents: foreign men – 191; foreign women – 147; foreign children – 76; Legation residents: Chinese men – 180; Chinese women – 107; Chinese children – 69; a total of 883 persons in all.

By now more news had reached Peking but it was frequently ambiguous and gave little to reassure the besieged. As Mary Andrews wrote on 31 July, 'All sorts of reports are coming in all of the time of the movements of the troops, but we do not know at all what to believe. Today our troops are reported at Chang-Chia-Wan, ten miles from Tung cho.' This news was incorrect as the relief force was still at Tientsin, as a letter which arrived on 1 August confirmed; it stated that the force would not now depart until 28 or 29 July, the delay being caused by failure to secure transportation of supplies, and more importantly, many of the foreign contingents were not expected to reach China before the

beginning of August. Word had also reached Tientsin that the ministers and their families in Peking had all been wiped out, therefore removing the need for a swift advance on the capital. News of the actual situation reached the allied command at the end of July from a messenger who managed to break through the Chinese lines.

On 2 August a letter arrived in Peking written by Lieutenant-Colonel J.S. Mallory of the 41st US Infantry on 30 July; it stated: 'A relief column of 10,000 is on the point of starting for Peking, more to follow. God grant they may be in time.' Another dispatch on the same day brought encouraging news to the besieged that the foreign settlement at Tientsin had been relieved, that Seymour's expedition had been safely brought back, and that two arsenals and Tientsin City had been captured.

The situation in Peking was one of contrasts. In certain areas of the perimeter, the Chinese kept up a steady fire. Those in the Fu, the Hanlin and in the Mongol Market on the west part of the wall and to the east of the French Legation were still very hostile while those to the east of the German Legation and on the east part of the wall appeared to be quite friendly. Here the German and Chinese positions were separated by a loopholed wall seven or eight feet high and about two feet wide. The Tsungli Yamen was continuing its exchange of communications with the besieged and two edicts were issued, one of which commanded Jung Lu to provide an escort to Tientsin for the ministers. A number of Chinese soldiers came up to the eastern barricades on 4 August talking openly about escorting the foreigners to Tientsin. On 5 August the Yamen sent in word to the Italian minister that King Humbert had died.

There was still scepticism about such friendly overtures particularly as the Chinese were continuing to build fortifications and saps. On

RIGHT **Walls of Peking and the An-Ting gate, which was captured by the British in 1860 and which overlooks the Summer Palaces, which were destroyed in the rebellion. The average height of the walls of the Tartar City was 50 feet and the average width 40 feet. Every 40 or 50 yards were buttresses. They were built mainly of huge bricks and concrete. After the Boxer rebellion, they were demolished. (Anne S.K. Brown Military Collection, Brown University Library)**

BELOW, RIGHT **On the walls of the Tartar City in a photograph published in July 1900. Possession of the top of the Peking walls by American troops was the salvation of the Legations. The Chinese barricade was in the immediate foreground and the American position was in the middle distance. To the left was the Legation Quarter. (Anne S.K. Brown Military Collection, Brown University Library)**

9 August the German ex-captain, von Strauch, heard sounds in the Mongol Market and went to the Russian Legation where he could look down the western line of defence. He found the Chinese digging a ditch with the evident idea of undermining the allied barricade. The Nordenfelt gun was turned on them and a marine contingent charged, driving them back. A bag of powder and a fuse were found in the ditch. Von Strauch took the opportunity of enlarging the perimeter here by occupying and fortifying some houses. On the next day four Boxers were discovered in the same vicinity and attacked, provoking a general attack that was the fiercest since before the truce.

Food was now becoming critical and it was proving difficult to feed all of the Chinese converts in the Fu. A few days earlier, the ministers had asked the Tsungli Yamen to supply some food but as no word was heard from it, extreme measures had to be taken which involved killing stray dogs. The makeshift hospital was still receiving casualties from gunshots, and a number of infants and children had succumbed due to sickness brought on by poor nourishment, the extreme heat and other conditions. Fortunately there were five wells of good water and two of bitter water within the compound.

During the day, there was little firing but on several evenings the besieged were exposed to short periods of rapid firing from the Chinese lines and they responded with the Nordenfelt. A new barricade was built across the canal near the British Legation and the Austrian Maxim gun was mounted there. This was a precautionary measure against a general Chinese attack up the dry bed of the canal from the Imperial City wall which could have easily carried the Legation gate. So quiet had things become during the day that several ladies were allowed to visit the stretch of city wall held by the Americans on 10 August. At no time were they exposed to enemy fire as the area had been so effectively barricaded. The Chinese Christians had excavated the city walls for the bricks and laid hundreds of yards of barricades on the city wall, some crosswise, some lengthwise and some guarding the sloping zigzag path down from the 60-foot wall.

While on the wall, the ladies heard a marine shout up to a colleague on the wall, 'Foreign troops forty miles away'.

The Relief Column

On 4 August the second relief column numbering approximately 17,000 men had moved out of Tientsin in the direction of Peking. Lessons had been learnt from Seymour's failed expedition and it was decided to take an alternative route following the Peiho River rather than the railway line. This would allow the force to bring additional supplies by boat. The force was under the command of British General Sir Alfred Gaselee, in place of the German Field Marshal, Count von Waldersee, who had not yet arrived in China. It consisted of 2,900 British troops, 2,200 American troops with six guns and a total of 9,000 men and 24 guns from the Japanese 5th Division. In addition the

A 3-in. gun of Light Battery 'F', 5th United States Artillery commanded by Captain Henry J. Reilly, in action at Yangtsun at 1.00pm on 6 August 1900, during the advance on the capital, photographed by C.F. O'Keefe. Reilly was killed on 15 August during the futile attack on the Forbidden City. (Jean S. and Frederic A. Sharf Collection)

Russians sent 2,900 men, two batteries of artillery and one squadron of cavalry, and the French 1,200 men and 12 guns. Additional forces, mostly sailors, came from Germany, Italy and Austria, but lacking transport were forced to return to Tientsin around 7 August. A further 23,000 men, mostly Japanese and Russian troops, were left to guard Tientsin, the Taku Forts and the railway line.

Opposing them were as many as 80,000 Chinese Imperial troops made up of Braves, Greens and Bannermen, although the only real resistance was expected to come from the 1st and 2nd Divisions, one of which had already lost its leader, General Nieh, at Tientsin. Defending the approaches to the capital were Tung's 4th Division and the 5th or Headquarters Division under Jung Lu which also possessed most of the artillery. While the 4th were considered hostile, the political allegiance of the 5th was unknown. Where the Boxers were was unclear but they had ceased to be a factor. As word of the relief column reached Peking, Chinese troops headed south to oppose them. At Yangtsun were 20,000 troops under General Sung while a further 10,000 commanded by General Mah headed for Peitsang.

For the first day or two conditions were bearable and the force easily captured the Hsiku (Si-ku) Arsenal on Sunday, 5 August, but had a stiff fight with the Imperial troops at Peitsang, where the Chinese had built extensive earthworks and trenches. The allies advanced shortly after 4.00am and within an hour had taken the forward trenches. Nonetheless, the enemy put up a stiff resistance and the Japanese contingent alone had over 300 casualties. The fight had lasted over seven and a half hours. On the following Monday, the Chinese were located at Yangtsun. Private Harry Dill of the 14th US Infantry noted that this engagement was particularly severe and the allied force was under a heavy fire for two hours. 'The rifle balls were coming like rain, throwing up little puffs of dust, and the shrapnel was dropping everywhere. I saw one shell knock over 16 men, though only seven were injured … we advanced with a yell and were for nearly three-quarters of an hour in the open where we encountered an awful fire. We pressed on, however, and carried the trenches at the point of the bayonet. Some of the men were overcome by the heat and a few went raving insane.' His unit lost 14 killed outright and 56 wounded, some of whom died later. The other troops were British and they lost 11 killed and over 30 wounded.

On 9 August Chinese forces were located at Hosiwu but were dispersed by the 16th Bengal Lancers and a long-distance artillery bombardment. The Chinese had been attempting to cut a large channel to the river with the object of flooding the countryside and preventing the allied transport junks from moving further north. Fortunately for the allies, they had been stopped before they had completed their plan.

There was practically no further opposition until Peking was reached but already the men were exhausted; they were allowed several extra hours of rest on 10 August before setting off later in the day. Conditions had deteriorated rapidly and the marching had become almost unbearable with temperatures reaching 104°F with no cloud cover or wind. On Sunday, 12 August Tungchow was reached and easily taken. The town was found to be deserted as the Imperial troops had quit the place leaving some Boxers to roam at large before they, too, departed prior to the arrival of the allies. The only action was the destruction of the South Gate of the town by Japanese artillery.

Following an inter-allied conference at Tungchow, a reconnaissance was ordered in the direction of the capital with the plan that the whole force would concentrate on the 14th and attack Peking on Wednesday 15 August. It was to be a well-executed operation and Gaselee did not want any one contingent trying to outdo the other. The Russians would have none of that, however, and said their whole force would move out on Tuesday but not before. However, on the evening of Monday the 13th they quietly moved out troops in the hope of capturing Peking themselves.

THE RELIEF OF PEKING

Since the siege began, the Chinese had been split into two factions – those that supported the Boxers and the rebellion, and those who were opposed to it. There was constant wrangling in the Tsungli Yamen and two of the ministers who had tried to persuade the Empress Dowager not to besiege the legations were beheaded on 3 August. The appointment of an extremist, Li Ping-hung, to assist in the defence of the capital was a blow to the moderates and it was no coincidence that shortly after his appointment the truce ended. With leaders sympathetic to the Boxer cause in command, the Chinese showed a renewed determination to repel the foreign force which was approaching the city.

The allied plan called for the force to advance westwards in four main columns paralleling the Imperial Canal but each contingent would take a different route to Peking and attack a different sector. For the Russians on the right (or northern flank), the task was to attack the Tung Chih Men; the Japanese following the paved road which ran north of the canal were to assault the eastern gate of the Chih-Hua Men and the walls of the Imperial City. South of the canal and on the extreme north-east corner of the Chinese City lay the Tung Pien gate, which would be the American target. And further south along the eastern wall of the Chinese City lay the Hsia Kuo gate, the designated point for the British contingent on the southern flank. The French contingent was assigned the position in between the Japanese and Americans.

Unfortunately, the premature movement of the Russians out of their position on the night of 13 August resulted in a change of plan, Gaselee writing, 'the intended concentration was abandoned, and the troops

THE RELIEF OF PEKING

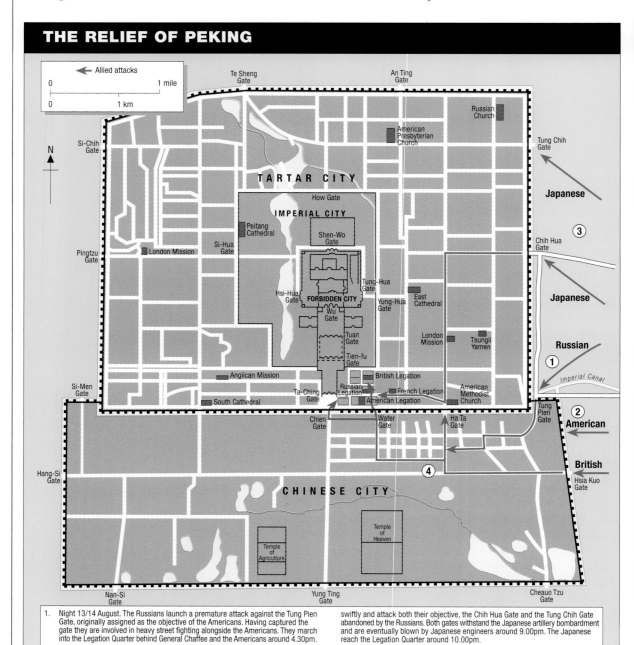

1. Night 13/14 August. The Russians launch a premature attack against the Tung Pien Gate, originally assigned as the objective of the Americans. Having captured the gate they are involved in heavy street fighting alongside the Americans. They march into the Legation Quarter behind General Chaffee and the Americans around 4.30pm.

2. At daylight Chaffee's Americans march to the sound of the gunfire. They now have no gate to attack and instead assault the wall between the Tung Pien and Hsia Kuo gates. Bugler Calvin P. Titus wins the Congressional Medal of Honor for scaling the walls single handed and unarmed. The Americans fight their way through to the Legation Quarter at around 4.40pm.

3. Responding to appeals for assistance from the Russians, the Japanese advance swiftly and attack both their objective, the Chih Hua Gate and the Tung Chih Gate abandoned by the Russians. Both gates withstand the Japanese artillery bombardment and are eventually blown by Japanese engineers around 9.00pm. The Japanese reach the Legation Quarter around 10.00pm.

4. The British begin their attack last having further to advance than the other contingents. They assault the Hsia Kuo Gate around noon. Resistance is minimal and the Royal Artillery blast a hole in the gate. Moving through the Chinese City a detachment of 7th Punjab infantry are sent towards the Hata Men. Men of the 7th Rajputs clear the Water Gate and enter the Legation Quarter at around 2.40pm. The rest of the column breaks in through the Chien Men.

Russian soldiers at Tung Pien Men gate, Peking, on 14 August 1900, photographed by C.F. O'Keefe. It was the wrong target and the Russians had a hard fight lasting 14 hours before they overcame all resistance. This view is looking south at the gate of the Chinese City through which the Russian troops entered Peking. (Jean S. and Frederic A. Sharf Collection)

'The Severe Fight of the Great Japanese Army: Illustration of the Fall of Peking'. A coloured woodblock print drawn by Toshimitsu, printed on 15 August and published on 18 August 1900 by Katada Chojiro. That this picture was printed the day after the relief of Peking suggests that this and other prints were prepared in advance in anticipation of the victory. (Anne S.K. Brown Military Collection, Brown University Library)

were all hurried forward to assault the city of Peking'. The allied generals decided to move the attack up to 14 August and all the contingents were in position by the evening of the 13th ready to attack the next morning. Around midnight on the 13th, firing was heard in the direction of the Tung Pien Men and it was determined that the Russians had moved diagonally across the allied front and attacked the wrong gate. Apparently Russian scouts had noticed that the sector around the Tung Pien gate was lightly held and decided to attack it. Whether or not this movement was deliberate, the Russians simply mistaking one gate for another, they nonetheless were successful in their endeavour. Under General Vassilievski, the Russian detachment advanced across a narrow bridge over the moat and killed all the Chinese in the outer gatehouse. Next they brought up two guns which bombarded the iron-sheathed gate and breached it.

By now the Chinese had been alerted and were firing down from the wall, but in the darkness and a heavy rainstorm could not see the enemy below. It was a different situation when the first Russians entered the courtyard between the outer and inner gate. A blistering fire from the walls poured into the Russians but despite heavy casualties they were soon in control of the Tung Pien Men, which they occupied until the main force came up at 10.00am the following morning.

Japanese troops who had moved out at daybreak on the 14th bore the brunt of the fighting when they assaulted the Chih Hua Men, losing 50 killed and 100 men wounded in an attempt to blow in this gate. They withdrew and kept up a constant but futile bombardment with their 54 guns for the rest of the day until nightfall when they finally got in around 10.00pm, having blown the gate with high explosives.

The Americans under General Abner Chaffee had moved out of camp at 5.00pm on 13 August having realised the situation. Led by the 14th Infantry commanded by Colonel A.S. Daggett, they advanced towards the wall south of the Tung Pien Men as they now had no gate to assault. When they reached the 30-foot wall, two companies of the 14th were pinned down by Chinese fire from the wall and the Fox Tower between abutments of the Chinese Wall near the Tung Pien. There was no alternative but to scale the wall and volunteers were asked for. Trumpeter Calvin P. Titus stepped forward and offered to climb the wall. Using his fingers and toes to find jagged holes in the masonry, he ascended to the top to find it undefended. Captain Learnard, the regimental adjutant, came next; he was followed immediately by other troops who then hauled up their rifles and ammunition pouches on a rope made of rifle slings. While they were climbing, the Fox Tower burst into flames from artillery fire from Reilly's Battery. Sydney Adamson, the Special Correspondent and Artist in China for *Leslie's Weekly*, was an eye-witness to the event: 'I watched these men of H Company as they

The desperate dash of American Marines along the walls of Peking, depicting an attack upon the Chinese barricades on the Tartar City Walls, in a drawing by Gordon Grant from a description cabled by Sydney Adamson and published in *Leslie's Weekly* on 15 September. This sortie enabled a gate to be opened to admit troops of the allied relief force on 15 August 1900. (Anne S.K. Brown Military Collection, Brown University Library)

The Water Gate under the wall of the Tartar City, Peking, photographed by the Royal Engineers. A few days before the assault, a message had been sent out of the Legation compound telling Gaselee of this gate and advising him to enter the Tartar City and make his way through the side streets to this opening. British troops entered the city on 14 August 1900 by means of this gate. (Jean S. and Frederic A. Sharf Collection)

scaled the walls and listened to the bullets cracking as they struck the stone or whistled clear in the sunny air, and I wanted to yell in sheer excitement. I had been in a cavalry fight that morning, when the air fairly buzzed with bullets, and when the fire opened on our right and rear we had to retreat; I had seen forty odd Japanese field guns pouring in a deadly hail of missiles to the Tartar City; but this was the best of all; the true spirit was here. It made one's blood tingle to see each man feel his way up, till he reached the last, most difficult place, and then was grasped and pulled over the parapet, ready to add another musket to those cracking along the wall.' As more troops mounted the wall up an improvised ladder constructed out of bamboo poles, the Americans planted their flag around 11.03am and moved off in the face of continued Chinese fire to assist the Russians who were still fighting in the courtyard and neighbouring streets of the Tung Pien Men.

Around noon on the 14th, the British moved towards the Hsia Kuo Men, which was found to be empty, the garrison having fled. Lieutenant Roger Keyes of the Royal Navy described what happened next in a letter written from Peking on 6 September: 'We pushed on and after a brief slight skirmish battered in the East gate of the Chinese City, went along parallel to the Tartar City wall through the Chinese City, crossed the canal or drain bed at the water sluice gate under the legations under a heavy but ill-directed fire and into the legations at 2.30pm.'

Following the breaching of the gate by the Royal Field Artillery, Keyes himself had scaled the wall and hoisted the white ensign from his ship, HMS *Fame*. General Gaselee had a brief surprise when he saw the allied flags blowing in the wind from the walls but then a signaller appeared and with his semaphore flags sent the message: 'Come in by sewer' and pointed to the wall beneath him. In the seven-foot-high tunnel, American marines and men of the 7th Rajputs removed gate bars and other debris and shortly after 2.40pm entered the Legation Quarter.

For the besieged themselves Tuesday 14 August had started like any other day with more firing from the enemy. During the morning the Chinese were sending in shells from the wall to the north of the British Legation, one of which exploded in MacDonald's dressing room, another killed a German in the German Legation, and several defenders were slightly wounded including an American Marine, Mitchell, whose arm was badly shattered by a bullet which came through the loophole by 'Betsy' which he was manning. On the previous evening, some of the heaviest firing had been experienced with at least six separate attacks beginning around 8.00pm and coming from the west. The besieged responded with their Maxim, Nordenfelt, the Italian 1-pdr. and old 'Betsy' while the American Colt was in front of the Legation. Luella Miner noted in her diary on the 13th, 'Sometimes there would come a lull of five or ten minutes, then the bullets would shower in again, some estimated at the rate of a hundred and twenty a minute. As they began before dark and kept it up until daylight, with a cannon on the wall near the German Legation throwing three-pound shell for variation, it was not especially soothing.' However, the tone of her diary entry changed on the following day when she wrote, 'At last our ears have heard the sweet music for which we have been listening for two months – the cannonading of the relief army – so plainly that we know the intense

Facsimile of a drawing entitled 'The first entry of British-Indian troops into the City of Peking, by Schönberg reproduced in the *Illustrated London News* on 24 November 1900. The scene depicts Major Scott of the Royal Engineers leading the way under the Water Gate towards the Legation Quarter. The mud was so thick here that the Indian soldiers sank up to their waists but there was no opposition from the Boxers. (Anne S.K. Brown Military Collection, Brown University Library)

Schönberg sent this sketch to his paper along with the following note: 'Almost the first to enter Peking was Captain Soady and his detachment of Sikhs. On reaching the top, Captain Soady unwound his turban and waved it as a signal to the rest of the British soldiers, who opened the inner gate.' (Anne S.K. Brown Military Collection, Brown University Library)

desire and imagination are not deceiving us, as so many times before. Our deliverance is at hand.'

The Indian troops poured in through the sluice gate and up Canal Street and arrived at the British Legation. Civilians came rushing out and showered the Indians with kisses. For Keyes, what met his eyes came as something of a surprise: 'It looked like a garden party. All the ladies looked nice in clean white and light-coloured dresses, strolling about on the lawn. Some of the men who had run in from the barricades looked rather fierce with arms of sorts festooned round them but most were in flannels having a quiet afternoon off … they all wanted to shake hands with us.' Even though the occasional bullet and shell whizzed overhead, most of the opposition had faded away. The Americans reached the Legations around 4.30pm and an hour later came the Russians under General Lineivitch. The Japanese led by General Fukushima were delayed because they had not only attacked the Chih Hua Men but also the Tung Chih Men, the original target of the Russians, and did not reach Legation Street until nightfall. The first French troops reached the Legation Quarter on 15 August.

Peking had been relieved – but there was one place which was still under siege, the Peitang Cathedral. Relief did not come to the tiny garrison until 16 August when 1,200 allied troops made up mostly of Japanese troops, overwhelmed the Chinese attackers. The reporter of the *Shanghai Mercury* described the situation: 'When I reached the Imperial City gate a little after nine on the 16th, the French were still pouring shells through the gate, but hesitated to march in. Along with a few others I climbed over the Imperial walls and entered the Cathedral grounds by a side entrance. There was very little resistance to our troops, and so they marched on past the entrance to the Cathedral into the Palace grounds north of the Palace. There were fired a few shots by the Chinese along the street, but none from the palace quarters.'

At one stage during the siege the cathedral had endured 28 consecutive days of shelling, four days more than the whole period in which any of the Legations were shelled. To defend the building, the French had 2,000 rounds of ammunition, the Italians less. Whenever one of the garrison had fallen, his place had immediately been taken by a native Chinese. A number of explosions were detonated, killing and wounding many, and the adjacent Foundling Hospital was completely wrecked. Of the 42 Italian and French sailors who helped to defend the cathedral, six Italians and four Frenchmen along with their young Breton officer, Paul Henry, were killed, and one officer and 11 men wounded.

The besieged in the Legation Quarter had sustained a relatively small number of casualties during the entire period of the siege; the figures would have been far greater had it not been for the well-constructed barricades and defences. Their only meat in the final weeks had been

mule and pony but they had a good supply of brown bread and plenty of rice. According to one estimate, casualties among all volunteers during the siege was 67 killed or died from wounds, and 167 wounded; casualty rates among servicemen from the eight nations was four officers and 49 men killed, nine officers and 136 men wounded. In Roger Keyes' estimation, 'As long as they could keep off starvation I don't think there was the slightest chance of their being captured; the Chinese – though plucky in defence – haven't got it in them to attack. And the Legation is so excellently placed it is almost impossible to shell it except from a very near distance, which the Chinese didn't seem to realise.'

While the main scenes of the Boxer rebellion were Peking, Tientsin and Taku, it has to be remembered that throughout 1900 and particularly during the sieges, many incidents were taking place away from the large centres. In Manchuria, Boxers had ripped up lines and destroyed the railway station at Chailar, and there was hard fighting

'The Fall of Peking: Illustration of the Flight of Enemy Generals'. Woodblock print drawn by Toshimitsu and published in October 1900 by Katada Chojiro. A typical Japanese print of the period, it is almost identical to prints depicting the Sino-Japanese and Russo-Japanese wars. (Anne S.K. Brown Military Collection, Brown University Library)

The ruins of the Student Interpreter's House within the British Legation compound as it appeared after the siege in a photograph by the Royal Engineers. During the siege, it was home to the German and Japanese legations. The former occupants, the student interpreters, were praised for their efforts in the defence: 'They behaved with pluck and dash, yet a steadiness under fire worthy of veteran troops.' (Jean S. and Frederic A. Sharf Collection)

Ruins of the Legation Quarter, Peking, in a photograph taken by a member of the Royal Engineers following the relief of the Legations. The siege had laid waste to most of the city and when the foreigners were finally able to walk around, they were appalled by the desolation and destruction brought about by fires and bombardment. (Jean S. and Frederic A. Sharf Collection)

between Chinese troops and Russians especially at Aigun, where a two-day battle ensued. While the allies were busy engaging Chinese forces in the main theatre, there was nobody protecting those unfortunate not to have been able to flee to the relative safety of Peking. Many atrocities were inflicted on western missionaries and their families, while others managed to escape following near-fatal experiences. Estimates of casualties among missionaries and civilians in the provinces varies. One estimate gives the figure at around 200 missionaries and more than 50 children murdered between 31 December 1899 and 5 October 1900. Following the relief of Peking, the allies took excessive reprisals against the perpetrators of many of these atrocities, in many cases executing innocent Chinese.

Peking was devastated. Lieutenant Holbroke of the 26th Baluchistan Regiment wrote to his father on 23 August that 'Peking is mostly in ruins. The Legations are absolutely in ruins. I don't know how they managed to hold out so long – they were eating mules and dogs.' Private G. Haywood of the 3rd Battalion of the Rifle Brigade noted in his diary on 16 August that the Legations and roads adjoining presented a sight never to be forgotton: 'Across the roads was barricade after barricade every 20 yards or so. Every building left standing was sandbagged up to the roof. The only buildings left standing were in the British and American Legations, the Hong Kong Bank and Hotel de Pekin.' Jasper Whiting, an American war correspondent working for the *Westminster Gazette*, arrived a few weeks later and observed what he saw: 'When we entered Peking we found the city swarming with foreign troops but deserted by the Chinese. Evidence of shot and shell and fire were to be seen on all sides. Acres upon acres of a once thickly populated city had been burnt to the ground. Temples and palaces were pierced with shells or destroyed, and miles upon miles of houses had been sacked of all things valuable they once contained … nothing foreign remains uninjured; even the British Legation bears innumerable evidences of the frightful state of affairs which has existed. Cannon are planted over the gates of the city; breastworks have been thrown up; everywhere are fortifications. Even on the walls of the Legations are many impromptu barricades.'

AFTERMATH

Hole created in the wall of the Imperial City by British Troops as it appeared in a photograph by the Royal Engineers. This hole was very close to the British Legation compound. Two companies of the Royal Welch Fusiliers were sent to hold the Llama Temple in the Forbidden City about half a mile from the British Legation but a hole first had to be made in the south wall to allow access. (Jean S. and Frederic A. Sharf Collection)

Most of the fighting in Peking ended on the 14th, but on the following day the American forces advanced to attack and occupy the Imperial and Forbidden cities, from whose walls the Chinese were still firing sporadically. The American commander, General Chaffee, had not yet received an order from the American government that with the Legations relieved no American troops were to take any further aggressive action. In the attack on 15 August one gate was blown in and the troops poured into a courtyard dominated by a tower over another set of gates from which the Chinese began firing. The Americans returned fire and brought up guns to knock down the gates. This process was repeated several times gate by gate. Faced with the final gate before the Forbidden City the US troops received the order to withdraw. General Chaffee was furious. Casualties had been suffered, among them the redoubtable Captain Reilly of the artillery who was killed by a sniper around 9.00am. The Forbidden City was not entered by the allied forces until 28 August.

As allied guns were still hammering away at the walls and gates on 15 August, the Dowager Empress disguised as a peasant women, accompanied by the Emperor, some Grand Councillors and various other members of the court, climbed on some rickety carts and fled northwards out of the capital. Over the next two months this retinue, which gradually grew in size, wandered from place to place covering a distance of 700 miles before settling at Sian, the capital of Shensi Province, in late October. According to one Chinese observer, Chuan Sen, an assistant professor in the Imperial College, shortly after the escape of the Dowager Empress, Prince Ch'ing, knowing that the city could not be defended, distributed flags of truce to the Chinese soldiers and ordered them to be put on the city wall. The Empress did not return to Peking until 6 January 1902.

However, on 3 September 1900 Prince Ch'ing and Li Hung-Chang returned to Peking invested with the full powers to act as Plenipotentiaries in dealing with the allied powers to arrange a peace settlement. On the day of Prince Ch'ing's arrival, Fred Whiting, the artist for the London *Graphic*, noted the scene: 'He was met some three miles away from the North Gate of the city by a detachment of Japanese cavalry. While at the gate, where his soldiers were disbanded, a detachment of the 4th Bengal Lancers was waiting to take its place in the procession … Prince Ch'ing wore ordinary Chinese costume, not even wearing his red button cap and peacock feathers – the signs of high rank.'

The last vestige of Boxer resistance in Peking collapsed on the same day the Empress departed, when the Peitang Cathedral was finally relieved. Thereafter the soldiers of the allied armies were free to roam the city plundering and looting whatever took their fancy. Even the

ABOVE, RIGHT **Funeral Service for Captain Henry J. Reilly, 5th United States Artillery, as photographed by C.F. O'Keefe. Reilly was killed in action on 15 August 1900 and buried at the US Legation on the following day. He was fifty-three when he died and was a veteran of the Spanish-American War, where he saw action in the Santiago campaign. During the advance on Peking, his battery was involved in the actions at Yangtsun, Hosiwu and Matau. (Jean S. and Frederic A. Sharf Collection)**

ABOVE **Li Hung-Chang, the Chinese official who was selected to negotiate a peace settlement with the allies although he was described at the time as a 'wily old Mandarin … there is good reason for believing that he has been in constant communication with the Empress and Boxer chiefs all through the disturbances'. This photograph was taken in Hong Kong on his way to Shanghai and was published in September 1900. (Anne S.K. Brown Military Collection, Brown University Library)**

Legations participated, holding auctions of loot. The main event during the next few weeks was a grand parade held on 28 August by the victorious forces to impress their defeated foe. To drive their point home, the allies decided to hold their parade in the Forbidden City, sacrosanct in the eyes of the Chinese. Sydney Adamson, the correspondent for *Leslie's Weekly* and the *Evening Post*, described the moment: 'The British officers kept up their reputation as the cleanest, smartest, and best-horsed of all troops. In point of cleanliness in clothing and accoutrements, and in general bearing, the "Tommies" and the Indian troops were an easy first. When the Russian column filed through to the swing of a martial air we were all surprised to see that they were moderately clean. Then some of the Japs followed, headed by the general and staff. They were all smart and well uniformed.'

By now more and more foreign troops were swarming into Peking, which was almost devoid of the native population. Elsewhere villages and towns had been burnt and heavily looted by allied troops whose

ABOVE **Avenue of Statues, Ming Tombs, Peking, photographed by C.F. O'Keefe in 1901 and showing Troop L, of the 6th United States Cavalry on a sightseeing expedition. Following the relief of Peking, American troops served in the army of occupation until their departure from China in May 1901. (Jean S. and Frederic A. Sharf Collection)**

RIGHT **Bengal Lancers in action, from a drawing by Frank Feller. The lancers were an important arm of the allied force and were well suited to the open low-lying land of northern China. They participated in several of the punitive expeditions following the relief of Peking. (Anne S.K. Brown Military Collection, Brown University Library)**

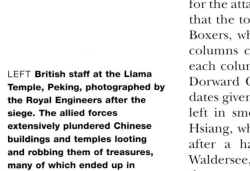

LEFT **British staff at the Llama Temple, Peking, photographed by the Royal Engineers after the siege. The allied forces extensively plundered Chinese buildings and temples looting and robbing them of treasures, many of which ended up in western museums. (Jean S. and Frederic A. Sharf Collection)**

only thought was for revenge. Any place suspected of showing anti-foreign sentiment was 'visited' by detachments of the allied force to teach the local inhabitants a lesson.

Between 8 and 25 September no less than four punitive expeditions were sent out, the first arriving at Tu Liu Ts'un, regarded as a centre of Boxer sympathy, 15 miles south-west of Tientsin. The Field Force Orders for the attack on this town stated that 'Information having been received that the town of Tiu Liu, 22 miles distant from Tientsin, is occupied by Boxers, who [have] long held their headquarters at that place, three columns consisting of troops as separately detailed in the orders for each column under the general command of Brigadier General A.R.F. Dorward CB, DSO will proceed to operate against that place, on the dates given in the detailed orders for each column'. The result – a town left in smouldering ruin. Three days later it was the turn of Liang-Hsiang, which was stormed and 170 of its citizens summarily executed after a hasty trial. After the arrival of Field Marshal Count von Waldersee, the supreme allied commander, at Taku on 25 September, these expeditions were stepped up. The German general commented that the only thing that worried him was 'our slackness with the

LEFT **Allied troops attacking Liang-Hsiang. This was a walled city located 18 miles south-west of Peking. The force that attacked the town on 11 September 1900 consisted of 800 Germans and 45 troopers of the 1st Bengal Lancers. Following a heavy bombardment, the Boxers fled in the process of which 30 were killed. (Anne S.K. Brown Military Collection, Brown University Library)**

BELOW, LEFT **Charge of the 1st Bengal Lancers sketched by Schönberg outside Tientsin on 19 August and reproduced in the *Illustrated London News* on 17 November 1900. The accompanying caption quoting from the artist's letter stated that, 'In this action thirty-seven prisoners were taken, of whom thirteen were "Boxers." Two hundred Chinese were killed during the fight.' (Anne S.K. Brown Military Collection, Brown University Library)**

Chinese'. Unfortunately, many innocent civilians were killed in the process as the allies pursued their vicious policy of punishing the population. Throughout the rest of 1900, expeditions were dispatched to persecute the former enemy, while executions of suspected Boxers and others implicated, such as the murderer of von Ketteler, continued.

In the south of China, particularly the Yangtse Valley, the occupation was more of a policing action to prevent the spread of anti-foreign sentiments, while in the north, it was decided to occupy the forts at Shanhaikwan at the terminus of the Great Wall. However, as the forts were very strong and believed to be well defended, it would require a number of heavily armoured ships to reduce them. A force of a dozen battleships and armoured cruisers was selected. The British gunboat *Pigmy* was sent to the fort bearing a delegation from Count von Waldersee to invite the Chinese commander, General Cheng, to surrender the forts for temporary occupation. They found that the garrison of 3,000 men was about to withdraw having already received word from the Russians at Port Arthur that they had dispatched

4,000 troops to occupy the forts. Cheng, fearing the arrival of the Russians, withdrew his garrison, leaving some crewmen of the *Pigmy* to man the forts. Upon hearing of the situation, Admiral Seymour sailed north on the *Alacrity* and arriving on 2 October, found the Russians outside the forts and the 18 men of the *Pigmy* inside. With diplomatic flair, Seymour managed to head off a confrontation by offering to share the forts among the allies. Shortly after, the flags of the seven allied nations were raised on one of the forts.

On 17 October, Waldersee arrived in Peking, and within a few days, Sir Claude MacDonald had departed the capital for a new posting in Tokyo, to be replaced by Sir Ernest Satow. The next day, a large allied force bore down on the city of Paotingfu, a hotbed of Boxer fanaticism. Failing to surrender to General Gaselee's requests, the town was invested and leading officials executed as reprisals for the murder of some missionaries. This was, Waldersee's method of sending a message to the Chinese and it received the full blessing of the Kaiser, although such excesses did not sit easily with all the allies. Von Waldersee continued to prosecute a harsh and vengeful policy against the Chinese into 1901. And he had the forces to do it. By 1 April 1901 the allied occupation force in China consisted of 300 Austrians, 18,181 British, 15,670 French, 21,295 Germans, 2,155 Italians, 6,408 Japanese, 2,900 Russians and 1,750 Americans; a total of 68,659 men.

On 26 February two prominent Boxer leaders were executed while others such as Prince Tuan were banished for life. Further Chinese opposition was rapidly withering, but by this time tensions were emerging between the occupying powers. On 12 March British and Russian troops almost came to blows over a railway siding in Tientsin. The Russians were the least popular and many feared that they had designs on Chinese territory in North China. The Germans were distrusted by the French and their commander, von Waldersee, was most unpopular, while the British were accused of not pulling their weight. Although clashing among themselves their policy towards the Chinese remained consistent. They were guided by three main objectives: the punishment of all Boxers and any Chinese officials viewed as having been sympathetic to their cause during the war; Chinese reparations to cover the cost of the allied expeditions; and all existing treaties were to be revisited to benefit the foreign powers. The Chinese delegation that had been nominated in September 1900 were presented with an eleven-point programme.

After much debate and revision of these conditions, the peace treaty was signed on 7 September 1901. It called for, among other things, the formal apology to Germany and Japan for the murders of Baron von Ketteler and Chancellor Sugiyama, the prohibition on arms and armaments entering the country, and the garrisoning of twelve places to safeguard communications. The Chinese were required to pay an indemnity of $333 million over a period of 40 years, In 1908, the United States government passed a resolution remitting to China its share of the indemnity in the form of scholarships for Chinese students, and in 1924 remitted all further payments.

But there was still the issue of access to China's markets and the allies took differing views on this ranging from the 'open door' policy as promoted by Britain, the United States and Germany, and the protectionist stance of nations such as Russia who wanted to establish spheres of influence in areas such as Manchuria in which Russian troops were already present on the pretext of policing the area. Japan also had her eyes on this region. A new treaty was signed with Britain in September 1902 which opened China up for even more trade. The following year saw Japan obtaining further concessions in the country, and the stage was set for a showdown between this upstart nation and Russia over Manchuria which flared up into full-scale conflict in 1904.

Some have seen the Boxer Rebellion as much as an uprising against the ruling Manchus as against the foreigners. As one writer put it, 'If the Boxer Uprising really was a "rebellion", against what constituted authority did the Boxers rebel? The answer can only be, the Manchu government of China.' To many Chinese, the Manchus were considered aliens to the country and the events of 1900 can be seen as a precursor

TOP LEFT **Field Marshal Count von Waldersee reviewing the allied troops photographed by the Royal Engineers. This review was held on New Years' Day, 1901, when the allied occupying forces paraded in front of the Imperial Palace. Von Waldersee himself played an insignificant part in the campaign as he arrived after the relief of Peking, but he was directly responsible for some of the reprisals against the Chinese as retaliation for the murder of von Ketteler and other civilians. (Jean S. and Frederic A. Sharf Collection)**

LEFT **Inspection of the Bengal Lancers by Count von Waldersee at the south-west gate of Peking, in a scene witnessed by John Schönberg. The German Field Marshal reviewed the lancers shortly after their return from an expedition. According to the caption in the *Illustrated London News*, 'the troopers presented a splendid appearance, and the Austrian attaché, General Hauptmann, said he had never seen such a fine body of men'. (Anne S.K. Brown Military Collection, Brown University Library)**

to the eventual overthrow of the Manchu Dynasty in 1912. Following the rebellion, the Manchu government had initiated a reform policy in 1902 and made plans to develop a limited constitutional government similar to the Japanese model. This was not enough and a coalition of Chinese students trained overseas, merchants and domestic dissidents began a series of uprisings in 1911, but the army applied only limited pressure and eventually came to terms with the revolutionaries. In February 1912, a revolutionary assembly in Nanking elected the first president of the Chinese Republic.

Throughout the next 30 years China continued to be plagued by foreign influence in certain parts of the country, particularly by the Japanese, who obtained the former German possessions following World War One. This friction between China and Japan burst into in full-scale war in the early 1930s and continued on and off until the end of the Second World War when China was finally able to throw of the shackles of foreign influence once and for all. Today, the Boxer Rebellion must be viewed with other revolts such as the Indian Mutiny or the Egyptian Revolt of 1882, as a nationalist struggle to overthrow encroaching colonial expansionism by Europe and the west, an expansionism based on ignorance of Chinese society, culture and religion.

THE BATTLEFIELD TODAY

The last century has brought major changes to China. Wars with Japan in the 1930s and 40s not to mention the devastating impact of the Cultural Revolution from 1949 onwards have obliterated many of the places connected with the Boxer Rebellion, although there are some vestiges still surviving. The main scene of the action, Peking (Beijing), has changed dramatically since 1900 and the Legation Quarter was completely transformed by the Chinese to make it safer and unrecognisable to those who lived there during the uprising. With a population of over ten million (it had just over one million in 1900), it consists of two parts: the old city, and new sections containing residences and industry surrounding the old city. As in 1900 the old city is divided into the Imperial City (or Tartar City) containing the Forbidden City, and the Outer (or Chinese) City. However the 15-metre walls which divided the old city and the nine gates which played a significant part in the siege of 1900 have been largely removed to make way for modern roadways and subway lines; there are one or two traces although these are some way from the old Legation Quarter. Some of the streets referred to in the various accounts survive such as Morrison Street as Wangfujing, one of the main shopping streets of Beijing, although much changed. The Outer City has particularly been affected by modern construction.

Of the various foreign legations, few remain. The Russian Legation building was bulldozed in the 1990s, while the Japanese Legation is now occupied by the Peking Municipality although the outside can be viewed. The canal which divided it from the British Legation can still be made out but it is now grassed over. The front gate of the British Legation still stands and the visitor can view it from the outside only, as the rest of the compound is out of limits as it is now home to the Public Security Bureau (PSB – the police). During the siege, the foreigners in the British Legation compound got their daily news, such as it was, from notices posted on a bell tower by Sir Claude MacDonald. This structure, which was erected in an open space near the main gate of the Legation to commemorate the Diamond Jubilee of Queen Victoria in 1887, still stands as a testimony to the courage of the besieged of 1900.

One major site connected with the siege is the Roman Catholic cathedral, the Peitang (Beitang in the pinyin system of transliteration), which withstood Chinese attacks for over 55 days in that long, hot summer of 1900; it still stands.

One of the conditions of the peace treaty was that a memorial should be built to commemorate the murder of Baron von Ketteler, and a white marble arch was erected by the Chinese government on the site of the murder but this was demolished in 1917 when China went to war against Germany. Ironically, by the time of its demolition, many Chinese considered it a memorial to the Chinaman who had killed von Ketteler! No other monuments or cemeteries survived the wars or desecration during the Cultural Revolution and have been built over. Other sites which were destroyed by the occupation forces following the end of the rebellion do have markers placed by the government, such as the ruined temples in the Fragrant Hills near Beijing.

The railway from Tientsin to Peking which Admiral Seymour followed is still in use but today a new expressway runs between the two cities.

Tianjin (formerly Tientsin) is still a major town up the railway from Peiho (Baihe) Bay. It too has undergone dramatic change but a reasonable amount of the early 20th-century city has been preserved by the city authorities, who view the old colonial buildings as part of the city's heritage and have taken steps to halt the progress of decay. Outside the former foreign settlements are other buildings such as churches which would have been standing in 1900. The forts at Taku (Dagu) which defended the Peiho River were demolished as one of the provisions of the 1901 Peace Treaty and there are no remains of the fortifications standing.

Of the various nations which participated in the relief expedition or had nationals involved in the siege or as missionaries in the hinterlands, several built memorials or added plaques to existing monuments. The Royal Marine Memorial near Whitehall in London, for instance, includes a representation of marines in action during the Peking campaign. In the United States, the China Relief Expedition as it was called came just after the Spanish-American War and during the Philippines Insurrection. In the years following many of the memorials to the war with Spain also included the Boxer Rebellion. At Oberlin College in Ohio, a memorial arch was dedicated in 1903 to the memory of the Oberlin Band, a group of 12 Oberlin graduates who went to China to establish opium refuges and clinics, opened schools and preached mainly in Shansi Province but were killed during the rebellion. Later a small plaque was attached in memory of the 30,000 Chinese Christians killed in the revolt.

FURTHER READING

For background to the Boxer Rebellion, two of the best sources are Peter Fleming's *The Siege of Peking*, London 1959, and particularly L.R. Marchant's introductory notes to *The Siege of the Peking Legations. A Diary* by Lancelot Giles, Nedlands, Western Australia, 1970. Both books along with Diana Preston's *The Boxer Rebellion: The dramatic story of China's War on foreigners that shook the world in the summer of 1900*, London 1999, provide excellent descriptions of the siege, the relief attempts and the subsequent events. One of the best accounts of the relief expedition, albeit from the American view, is A.S. Daggett, *America in the China Relief Expedition*, Kansas City, 1903. For a good overall contemporary account of the rebellion, see Arthur H. Smith's *China in Convulsion*, New York, 1901. The historiography of the rebellion, the rise of the Boxers, and their legacy is well laid out by Paul A. Cohen in *History in Three Keys: The Boxers as Event, Experience, and Myth*, New York, 1997.

The uniforms and costume worn by the belligerants during the Boxer Rebellion are discussed and illustrated in Lynn E. Bodin and Chris Warner's *The Boxer Rebellion*, London, Osprey, 1979.

There are numerous published diaries and first-hand accounts of the siege of the Peking Legations, making it one of the most chronicled events in Asian military history. Good examples include W.A.P. Martin, *The Siege of Peking*, London 1900, and the diary by Lancelot Giles referred to above; a recent compilation of some letters and diary accounts is Frederic A. Sharf and Peter Harrington's *China 1900. The Eyewitnesses Speak*, London 2000, which also includes an excellent bibliography of these sources. For the art generated by the rebellion, see Frederic A. Sharf and Peter Harrington, *China 1900. The Artists' Perspective*, London 2000.

INDEX

Figures in **bold** refer to illustrations